How A-CET came to Ethiopia

David Stables' Autobiography

How A-CET came to Ethiopia, David Stables' Autobiography was first
published in 2010 by A-CET, PO Box 8390, Leicester LE5 4YD,
England, UK.

a-cet.org

Cover design and layout by Flexpress.
Printed and bound in the UK by Flexpress.

Distributed in the UK by A-CET.

A catalogue record of this book is available from the British Library
Library of Congress Cataloguing in Publication Data available

ISBN 978-09557041-1-6

Chapters

Acknowledgements

Thanks to all of you who have encouraged me to write this book, particularly those who have taken time to read the draft and suggest alterations, or perhaps more wisely deletions. To those of you whose patience and understanding have borne with me through my outbursts of frustration and intolerance; I respect and value your support and friendship. Your names are too many to list, you know who you are and have my undying appreciation and thanks.

Images from Arthur Edwards of Sun Newspapers, Enigma Images, Filmmagic, Green Lions, Photo Kulubi, Publitek New Media and A-CET/EYES. Cartoons by Flantoons.

David Stables, Leicester, England, October 2010

Endorsed by Sir Bob Geldof

David Stables is a heroic man.
A council flat and state pension existence here in the UK.
In Africa the tireless, entrepreneurial godfather to countless bettered lives.

Bob Geldof

Bob Geldof
London
28th September 2010

Why this book?

Sometimes I'm encouraged and persuaded to tell stories from Africa or those other places I've worked in around the world. Yet often when I return from an overseas trip and respond to the "how was it?" question, I soon seen eyes glaze over as they complain about road potholes, poor rubbish collection or non working street lights. It's as if the "how are you?" question requires the bland response "I'm fine". Maybe this book will be like some talks I've given when an elderly audience in an over warm room has dozed off - old, tired, following a big meal or just bored. At least with this book, you can always put it down!

Often it's difficult to say how it really is, as so few have an in depth knowledge of how the non-tourist true Africa is or can really relate to even the most common overseas experiences.

Later friends and acquaintances have increasingly tried to cajole, almost bully, me to "write it all down". This I've tried to avoid, partly claiming lack of time, but mostly because deep down I value my privacy and I feel uncomfortable and shy about writing about myself. It seems rather pretentious to think that anyone could be at all interested in what I've done. But although this is about my life and how A-CET came to be, of necessity any autobiography is more about those other people who have touched and moulded my life.

Earlier writings, particularly on my experiences in conflict zones, put me back in to the trauma with recurring nightmares, so for some years I abandoned further writing until I felt stronger. It seemed best to forget those difficult periods. Finally persuaded again, here is my second attempt. An abridged autobiography composed of a selection of disjointed vignettes from my life. What to leave out has been more challenging than what to put in. Whilst I have tried to be as accurate as possible it is neither a travelogue nor a historical or cultural guide, just my views.

To initially refresh my failing memory I have read my letters and reports, looked through thousands of photographs and listened to tape recordings I've made, but most of this book has been written from memory, which is notoriously selective as one gets older. This collection of stories is generally arranged chronologically, as I know of no other way. For brevity some characters are an amalgam and some events have been compressed, so dates may be a bit vague. Occasionally some names have been changed to protect identities. These are my views as I remember them; if others feel omitted, misreported or unfairly recorded, apologies, but "If the cap fits" so be it.

I admit to little time for hypocrites and those who pretend to be what they're not, I have zero tolerance of corruption, cannot abide bullying or exploitation in any form and have little patience with fools. Waste is an anathema to me and our pathetic attempts at recycling in the developed world are at best an expensive joke. I have been accused of being indiscreet and undiplomatic, I prefer 'open' but will accept 'blunt'. Although some say, thankfully, time has mellowed me somewhat, what else can you expect of a Yorkshireman? A spade is, after all, a spade. As the saying goes, "You can always tell a Yorkshireman, but you can't tell him much".

Let this book help others understand what inner passion drives me. What I've written is neither to excuse nor justify and whilst I have no hidden agenda, I'll happily accept your donations for A-CET. This book may explain how I became what I am and why I do what I do. It attempts to say how my experiences have affected and shaped my character and personality and made me what I am today. Now I am what I am. To paraphrase the Sierra Leonean Krio saying:

"How you go know which side you go go, if you no go know which side you cum oot?"
("How can you plan your future, if you haven't understood or appreciated your past?")

My main motivation to write and publish this book has been that its sale will help to raise more funds to support the continuing work of the African Children's Educational Trust.

The more we do through A-CET, the more I see that there is to be done. Realistically I doubt if the educational needs of Ethiopia will be satisfied and their self sufficiency achieved in my life-time. For fuller details of A-CET's background, growth and activities and how you can help, please go to: **www.a-cet.org**.

Road block

Another routine day; already it was a sweltering hot and sticky morning as I drove from my beach house on the city outskirts to the industrial gas factory I managed. The blinding sun shone mercilessly from a clear blue sky, monkeys scurried around the palm trees and the birds were singing. Out of town I drove with the windows open, no air conditioning then, to get some cooling drafts into the car, although

already my shirt was sticking to my back and the car seat. I would change into a fresh shirt at the office. I hadn't noticed that there weren't the usual locals trudging or cycling into town, or that it was quieter than usual. I had already learnt the hard way not to wear a visible wristwatch or any rings, to keep nothing in my wallet except my ID card and a few Leone currency notes; my slim brief case was under my seat. Few cars in Sierra Leone had radios or cassette players. On rounding a blind bend there was an obviously hastily thrown together unaccustomed road block. We were nearing a barracks I passed every day. The road block was manned by crazed soldiers waving guns. I stopped and, on demand, proffered my ID card. This was studied initially upside-down until the photograph gave this illiterate beardless youth the clue how to read it. "Open boot" he screamed. This was an estate car, "Sorry no boot" I stupidly remarked as softly and calmly as I could. I must not antagonise these jumpy shifty-eyed guys and there didn't appear to be any officer or obvious leader about. Already I knew these soldiers were recruited on their inability to read or write, so that they could be easily indoctrinated and led unquestioningly. Before I could blink his rifle butt thwacked my cheek through the open window bringing tears to my eyes which mingled with the warm trickling blood and my sweat. "Open boot!" he screeched again, visibly nervous and nearly out of control at my seeming non compliance. I staggered out of the car and clutching the ignition keys opened the back of the car - which held nothing. Disappointed and after a nerve racking pregnant pause, he eventually shouted "Go". Gingerly I got back in my car, did a quick U-turn to go back home, glancing nervously in my rear view mirror for any wild shots.

This was a Sierra Leone 1971 attempted coup and it was a scenario I was to be an unwilling participant in and survivor of too many times and in too many countries over the next four decades. Here I had been foolish and had been extremely lucky; I had broken my own rule to never drive alone anywhere or at anytime.

If I were a cat, perhaps one of my nine lives was spent. So how did I get here?

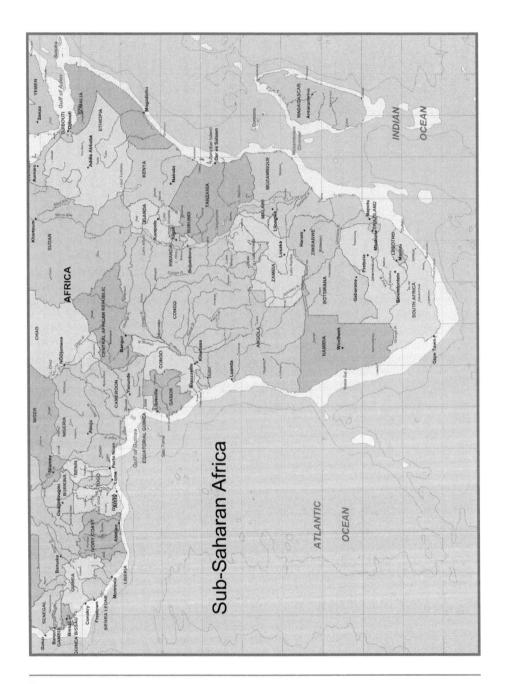

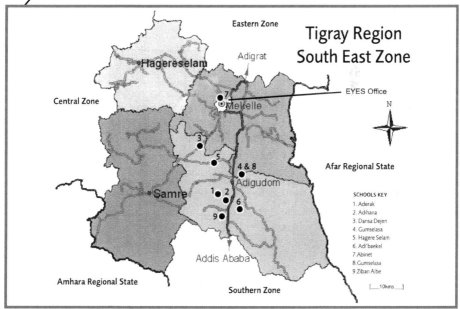

African Children's Educational Trust

Educating Ethiopians to develop Ethiopia

- A-CET is the small, effective, award winning, independent educational charity run by experienced dedicated unpaid volunteers, enabling thousands of vulnerable Ethiopian youngsters to develop themselves through education.

- We believe in every child's right to freely access appropriate quality education and, from decades of experience, know of a great need in Ethiopia where we work in liaison and cooperation with the local infrastructure.

- All Ethiopians are very keen on education and desperate to learn. They are highly intelligent and hard working.

- A-CET has two main programmes. One to support thousands of youngsters, mostly orphans, the abandoned or disabled through long-term care and modest financial scholarships. Two is helping communities to upgrade and build elementary schools.

- With our help, students get easier access to better education. This gives them more opportunities and choices and so, with financial security and better health they can increase their self-confidence. This improves their aspirations to reach their goals.

- We work through the local partner local registered charity Ethiopian Youth Educational Support (EYES) led by a small dedicated team of our trained and experienced ex-students.

- In building schools, we work at village community level, listening to their needs to support and guide their educational initiatives. Supervised and targeted giving at village level is highly effective with a high impact from which all benefit.

- A-CET is very careful how we spend your donations and all our projects become self-supporting. We do not tolerate waste and everything is accounted for in an honest, transparent and professional way. Where we work there is no corruption.

- There is so much talk of ending poverty. The way to end poverty is through education. We don't talk much, but act.

- With your help, we can change our children's lives in a very positive way for their and their families better future.

- We rely entirely on private voluntary donations with no Government support or funding. This is challenging, so please help us as much as you can. We can educate our students, giving them the knowledge they need so that they can develop their country.

- Whatever you feel you can contribute, will be greatly appreciated, thank you sincerely. Your support will help us to help change our youngsters lives. All donations are acknowledged, please be as generous as you can, thank you.

For further information please write to:

A-CET, PO Box 8390, LEICESTER LE5 4YD or go to: www.a-cet.org

A-CET is Registered Charity 1066869 (England & Wales)

Chapter 1 - School days

I was brought up the middle child in a 1930s semi with a large garden, set in a country lane north of Leeds, surrounded by fields and woods. My mother was a teacher and my father, whose parents thought he had married beneath him, was a Manchester economics graduate and a reluctant Chartered Accountant, rather than the historian he would have preferred. As was the custom then, we did not talk much, ever. I know why my siblings were christened Robin and Ruth, but never why I was David. Increasingly I realised that I must have been somewhat of a disappointment, at least to my father, not to have been their daughter, but she came later. We lived in a small village which lacked the cohesion of a church or school, but had a village hall, shops, post office, garage, inn and even a golf course. Now only the inn and golf course remain. During and just after the war the village hosted a prison camp full of White Russians, but it must have been a very open prison because the inmates worked on the surrounding farms. At Christmas the Russians held exciting parties for us children with home-made gifts for all. Many later intermarried and stayed on. We helped hay making and potato picking with horses and carts, and in the long holidays we wandered and played freely far from home for endless hours, collected coal from the rail tracks and fallen branches from the woods. We skinny-dipped in brooks and were vaguely aware of being leered at from afar by harmless old men. Food rationing was a part of life, we grew our own vegetables; food put out was instantly visually shared and whilst no scrap was left, we were never too hungry. I grew up well cared for, although I remember no touching or hugs; after all these were the forties. We had reasonable yet often repaired shoes and even wore underpants. I wore my older brother's cast off clothes which were probably "hand-me-downs" when he got them; this was usual at that time. Once at a next door birthday party I was given a pair of green shorts to wear; they were different from our usual drab grey and I suppose I hated being different. Quickly I managed to splash some dirty water from a bird bath on them hoping to be sent home to change; well I think it was water I spilt. What a wilful child I must have been. I was certainly sent home to change but, disgraced, not allowed to return to the party. Others at our school were not so well off, their clothes were patched and their homes had whitewashed walls; linoleum was a luxury. Some friends' houses I visited still lacked electricity or inside piped water.

Before we had bikes, we walked everywhere. In the winter of 1947 the snow was higher than I was in the paths cut through it. Primary School was a two mile walk from home

and held in a dusty, smoke filled/nicotine stained village hall that doubled at night for dances, cards and probably more. The urinals, full of soggy cigarette butts, as usual at that time, stank. We did everything in this same hall, including eating a hot lunch cooked on-site. At night all was packed away. School was interesting and learning was fun and I've always felt so much was practical and useful: country lore, handicrafts, poetry, traditional folk singing, spelling, essay writing and "sums". As a trained teacher mother sometimes came to school and read us stories; they must have been short staffed. We pressed wild flowers and collected rose hips and painted on old newspapers. We were taken on exciting trips, once to York, full of Roman remains, walls, castles, a captivating museum with a real old Victorian street and to climb the Minster towers. Here I discovered my own fear of heights which sent my knees weak and my head giddy. This is something I've lived with all my life and just have had constantly to force myself to overcome. We had a class mate with a cleft palate and another with epilepsy - they were just accepted and we knew how deal with the fits. In one school break a girl told me my mother had had a baby in a nursing home near her house. Undeterred that it was miles in the opposite direction to where I lived, after school I trudged off to visit. I was six and, being November, it was long dark when I finally made it back home to my frantic father. No telephones or late buses then, even if I'd had any money. Once a week after school I was sent for private piano tuition. Whatever my parents paid was wasted; the French tutor, "Mademoiselle" beat my knuckles mercilessly with the hard edge of her ruler for my tuneless strumming and many wrong notes. I was terrified and to my eternal regret I learnt little.

I must have been a very early National Health patient: I had my tonsils removed in the huge Leeds General hospital with its wards which seemed to stretch forever. The smell of chloroform or perhaps ether, shining stainless steel dishes, blood and custard are all confused. Some flash city kids relieved me of a rare chocolate bar (sweets were still on ration) that I had been given by Ma Needham, the village shopkeeper for whom I used to deliver the Yorkshire Evening Post after school. I was very trusting and can't have been very street-wise. I still had much to learn.

Initially as a Cub (Scout) "Bob-a-Jobber" I helped our local butcher and greengrocer for whom father kept the accounts and tallied ration book coupons. I found easy social skills using the telephone and dealing with customers. I operated a lethal bacon slicer and stuffed a sausage machine; mainly I recall with fat and bread crusts. I have early memories of the first bananas arriving in long wooden boxes, although there was more excitement when the first paper bags came, replacing old newspapers I'd previously cut up to wrap food. I re-trimmed and lightly sprinkled water on the vegetables as Dunhill the owner shouted *"fresh with the morning dew"!* I mucked out the stables and, standing on a stool, brushed down his horses, some of which he rode for fox-hunting and others for steeple-chasing. I enjoyed cleaning and polishing the horse tack by the tack room fire, that is when I could get the difficult wall mounted fire to light. One holiday he allowed me to set up a table by the road side and I sold cordial drinks, Tizer and fresh fruit, to cyclists panting up the long hill. I think my parents were not well pleased at my trading. This was my world, I felt useful and needed and I loved every minute of it. Life was fun and I had pennies in my pocket.

I have memories of being taken to an optician who filled my eyes with a liquid that seemed to blind me; alarmed I rushed to my mother. My eyes were OK although I was diagnosed with poor colour perception, something I have managed to live with or mask for most of my life.

Occasionally we took a week's holiday on the Yorkshire coast, travelling in the windowless back of one my father's company trucks and staying in bleak boarding houses run by fierce unwelcoming landladies. Once I was taken paddling and, realizing that in the middle of this pool I was unassailable, I refused to come out when called. *"OK we're off now"* one of my parents must have said; appalled at being abandoned was a good lesson and I rushed out. Staying with an Aunt in Kent with her two daughters, my cousins, was infinitely more fun. They had been visiting their father who worked in Colombia, South America, when war had broken out, and there they had stayed. Atlantic crossings for civilians must have been suspended. They were delightfully unconventional and wildly uninhibited, which I found exciting. We went in long echoing railway tunnels and screamed, a little eccentric for the rather repressed England of that time. In 1951 we visited the Festival of Britain and saw a 3D film which, sixty years later, is just coming back into vogue.

A spinster Aunt, in the days when the youngest daughter was taught little and expected to stay at home to look after her parents, was working in the Women's Volunteer Service (later WVRS) in the busy troop canteen on Harrogate station. She took me along. The canteen was steamy and smoke filled and I was told to collect up the empty tea-mugs. I must have been about seven and certainly very small, as I could hardly see over the table tops to know whether the mugs had tea in or not. Soldiers patted my head as I collected empty mugs and at the end of the day my pockets were bulging with big heavy pennies. Maybe these soldiers, still far from home, took me as their surrogate sons whom they had never seen. I learnt that a big disarming smile could produce dividends, although later this had the potential to cause embarrassment and misunderstandings. My Aunt wisely cautioned against my saying too much when I went home. Was this my first "secret"? I think this must have been the most exciting time of my sheltered Aunt's whole life and her greatest "freedom".

At primary school I never remember being coached or even told the day of our 11 plus selection examination, but I passed for Grammar School and was sent as a boarder to my father's old school, Queen Elizabeth I, chartered in 1591 in Kirkby Lonsdale, Westmorland. I loved every minute there, feeling it was like a holiday with school attached. In my first year I produced a winning play, compiled, edited and produced a cyclostyled news-sheet "One A Calling" - both firsts for a first year. I loved directing plays but it was never encouraged as a serious career choice. Food was sparse, breakfast often a half slice of fried bread smeared with Marmite or two thin tomato slices or powdered eggs - yet something must have been right as we grew strong on this. It was to be a long time before I ate a real egg from a shell. I was never much of a sportsman, with rotten hand/eye coordination, however I was a stoic long distance runner which I enjoyed and did moderately well at. This was a really good school with some quite modern concepts; since 1905 it had been mixed boarding and now it had a number of local day students. Every morning we were played classical music at assembly, in the evenings Gilbert and Sullivan when we read the spoken parts. The corridors were full of reproductions of well known traditional classic art. I became a choir boy and later head choir boy, loving singing and the ceremony of it all. We sang for George VI's funeral when the organ, playing long unused deep notes, sent clouds of fine dust out and had us all in fits of sneezing which developed into uncontrollable schoolboy giggling. Our humourless Music Teacher who doubled as Choirmaster was not best pleased. As a Boy Scout I later sold commemorative booklets for the Coronation of Queen Elizabeth II. At weekends we were shown full length classical, black and white films which are still memorable. We accepted and understood the discipline, but there was no fagging or bullying; we knew the boundaries and were encouraged to develop ourselves fully in many directions. But after three years, father fell ill, the money must have dried up and I returned home to be sent to the local grammar school.

I have already mentioned that I had worked for the local butcher and green grocer as a "Bob-a-Job" Cub, but later I worked for my own pocket money. From slicing bacon to serving customers at a very young age, I believe this was an important formative time. I delivered orders to the "big" houses and was certainly indulged with tips and hot rum-laced milk when delivering on cold winter days. It seemed a mile away from my home environment. I learnt my own worth, I was not too proud to do anything and I became increasingly confident at talking and dealing with all sorts of people. Maybe I was more than a little irritating and insufferably precocious. Importantly it gave me some money to get a bicycle and, with friends, go youth hostelling all over Yorkshire, the Lake and Peak Districts and North Wales. I once called on a school friend living in a remote North Yorkshire village. His father had just had a heart attack from which he later died. It seemed that only I knew what to do and how to use the one village telephone to call an ambulance.

By this time my father had lost his job and been blacklisted by his employers for refusing, as a Chartered Accountant, to "sign off" their accounts. Employment blacklists in the north were pretty much the kiss of death. Father was doing freelance book-keeping and auditing for a milliners and the odd sweet, tobacconist or corner shop - so much for his relatively high educational and professional qualifications. The Directors of the engineering company he worked for were apparently running an additional ghost sub-company and payroll to both cream off surplus profits and avoid taxes. Much later these Directors were arrested, tried, convicted and given lengthy custodial sentences. By then father had long since died of a heart attack in one of those long hospital wards full of moaning patients, often hidden behind screens or curtains, with that pervasive pungent smell of disinfectant. It took me many years before I could be persuaded to visit any hospital again.

I missed Queen Elizabeth School more than I realized at the time and never took to my new dull, uninspiring and humourless place where the rule was certainly conformism and to been seen but never heard. This day school was difficult to get to by public transport so I usually cycled the 20 miles there and back; I enjoyed that freedom. Living in the shadow of my academically brilliant elder brother, I rebelled and was always the badly behaved, undisciplined "disappointment". Students were treated with disregard and any initiative or individualism was arbitrarily and often brutally discouraged. My reaction was to challenge what I perceived as petty authority for authority's sake, something that has stayed with me throughout my life. I couldn't leave soon enough. I felt that I learnt little of use to fit me for any future life. One outstanding teacher far ahead of his time took us to visit other churches during their services: a Jewish synagogue, a Catholic church, Methodist chapels and the Unitarians, which I found fascinating. I cannot recall if there were any mosques at that time in Leeds. The only redeeming part of secondary schooling were two inspirational Geography masters, both well travelled ex-servicemen who made "overseas" sound fascinating. It was they who fired my imagination and life-long love of maps and with it my desire to travel. Together with Art, Geography was my best subject and I enjoyed these motivational teachers, who talked to and with you not at you. I loved copying or drawing maps and could spend hours pouring over an atlas which was more exciting than the encyclopaedias we had at home. But however hard I tried to study, basically I was unmotivated. Perhaps I was brashly over confident; I could talk to anyone and do anything asked or I set my mind to, and I could earn money. With that arrogance of youth, what did I need more schooling for? We had moved house to be near the hospital where father seemed to spend much of his time. It would have meant another new school for me and this didn't appeal. Even when top in something, I never got a prize - or was praised or encouraged. Were these happy care free days? I was happier to be free of them and their often mindless discipline imposed by despots. With me has stayed a feeling of great affinity with anyone who doesn't fit the mould of formal schooling. This feeling has never left me and constantly affects me now with what I currently do with educational charity A-CET. To leave school having just turned fifteen with only a selection of modest O levels was not the wisest decision, but given the same circumstances I would probably do the same again. If there was such a thing as a careers advisor, I never met one. Many of my aunts and cousins were teachers, but this never appealed to me. That throughout my life I was to become involved with teaching and education, which I found very satisfying, I cannot explain; was it in my genes?

I remember that questionable maxim: *"if you can't do it, teach it; if you can't teach it, teach the teachers to do it"*. I hope not.

My younger sister was about to start at a nearby grammar school. Money must have been tight at home and my mother went back to teaching. Holding only a Diploma she was ineligible to teach in a state school. For many years, until my sister graduated from University, mother taught sports and English in a private secondary school for rich girls with few academic pretensions.

I had written a short story for the children's section of the Daily Express which they published and sent me a half-crown postal order. Emboldened I wrote more. Although I was never published again I enjoyed writing. But to my eternal shame I had failed my General Certificate of Education in English Literature. This was not only a subject my mother taught but also I loved writing essays and reading books, poems and going to the theatre. We all remember a good teacher, also a bad one. Our English teacher was a veritable witch. Most of my life I seem to have been trying to catch up academically and constantly struggling to prove my worth. I got no career advice, except by inference that "art" was not a career and the army was no good if you were not rich; both quite incorrect, but then this school had pretensions of being academically oriented. Never being academically inclined I never felt I fitted at this school and this must have made me a rather subversive rebel.

I wanted to be independent; it was time to look for a proper full-time paid job.

Chapter 2 - Employment

During school breaks I had worked for a professional photographer uncle: "Ledbetter of Leeds" a modern new neon proudly proclaimed outside his offices. Bob was great fun, he had a full-size coal-fired steam traction engine that really worked and smelt exciting. How and why did Bob get a traction engine? During the war years even for commercial use vehicles were hard to come by and required completion of many forms which among details was what sort of vehicle was requested.

Apparently Bob ticked every box on the form and was "offered" this traction engine; a life-long lover of steam trains, he couldn't resist accepting this allocation.

I gather he started as a freelance ambulance-chasing photographer, but he claimed his later success was due to having taken photographs of the great and good slurping soup from their saucers during the 1930s opening of Leeds Civic Hall. Called by the Mayor, anxious to prevent the embarrassing publication of these offending photographs, he had to bring in the negatives, then on glass plates. There were threats of "never working again in Yorkshire" - that blacklist again. He brought the plates which were ceremonially smashed, and his photography business prospered. Twenty years after this event Bob showed me his original negative plates that he had kept as "insurance"; the smashed plates were copies. Bob worked as the stills cameraman at Carnforth Station for the seminal film "Brief Encounter"; although he claimed to have spent most of his time hosing pavements down to give that "just rained" effect. Bob was proud of his first motoring summons for dangerous driving, eating a sandwich and using the horn. Horns were really hooters mounted outside the cab and had to be squeezed. As well as industrial photography, Bob specialized in weddings. Colour photography was costly and rare, but he had an army of lady "tinters" who coloured in. At the weddings, in the back of his blacked out small van (I still must have been quite small) I developed these glass film plates and printed proof photographs. It was exciting, I felt useful, and the wedding food we got was a delight. These proofs were then shown to guests at the wedding reception with orders taken, advanced marketing indeed.

Leeds in the fifties was still clouded sometimes for days and weeks on end, in thick smoke-fueled fogs, clanking trams ran along tracks and steam trains were the norm.

I had also worked as a casual Christmas staff in the Leeds Post Office Registered Mail depot which involved lots of clerical work and, more excitingly, collecting mountains of mail bags from the railway station. At that time people posted unwrapped and un-plucked pheasants with just a label round the legs. Later, as a potential hotel management trainee, I worked in various capacities in a five star hotel on the Isle of Wight. This was a hotel definitely in the old style, with palm court and grand piano accompaniment to afternoon teas. In the restaurant I was serving red wine to a large round table with many guests. Next week I was told I would go onto to silver service and, anxious to learn, was watching an Italian waiter deftly serving a platter of cold meat salad when I noticed he uncovered a clutch of blue-bottle eggs under a meat slice when moving behind one guest. Fascinated how he would proceed I overfilled a wine glass until the starched crisp linen table cloth was totally awash with red wine. Next week I went onto silver service and learnt how to fillet sole at table. Serving one lady with her curry on a bed of rice she crossly complained that the beef stew she had ordered for her Pekinese was not also on a bed of rice. My first task was to take the Manageress's afternoon tea to her suite. The tray held dainty biscuits, a hot water pot and a milk jug covered with a lace and beaded doily. But the silver teapot on the silver tray held whisky. Probably too "pretty", I was pampered by rich old dowagers ostensibly ordering their midnight Horlicks; they knew exactly when the main kitchen formally closed and the regular kitchen staff left. To be fondled and drooled over by these old ladies, in return for crispy fiver tips was at best uncomfortable. Not as creepy though as the head barman who rather fancied me, requiring more than quick footwork to avoid. A "rejected lover" can prove very vindictive. I took care, smiled less and grew up fast. Favoured by the Manageress, my pay packet was a basic £3 a week but the 10% service charge from the restaurant, the bar and the lounge, all places where I worked, was over £40. However, I decided I was not quite ready for hotel work and I left with quite a lot of money. What I learnt about the hotel business was to prove very useful later in my life, particularly when I worked as a chef in an Oxford Cyrenian hostel for the homeless and managed my friend's 30 bedroom Hotel Merchantman in Plymouth, a place that would rival any immortalised by the TV series Fawlty Towers.

With full employment it was possible to literally walk into any job for which one applied. Lured like so many by a job title, the vacancy for a trainee surveyor attracted me. With it came vague dreams of involving myself in map making and perhaps my step towards overseas surveying. I took this job in the Estate Office of the recently nationalised canals. British Waterways was based in the old yet still profitable Aire & Calder Navigation Head Office in Dock Lane, Leeds.

My first job with the Waterways was to clear out a huge attic of "old documents" as they wished to convert it into a print room. It was full of dusty stacks of huge leather bound gilt embossed books some over a meter wide. They seemed to be the original plans for new canals which from the mid 1760s were becoming the vogue. As with railways and later motor-ways, initially there was much public opposition to this perceived spoiling of the rural idyll. These were really beautiful books and it seemed so terrible to throw them out. I asked and was allowed to keep one smaller book and shared it with my Uncle Bob the photographer who particularly loved old maps almost as much as I did. Thirty years later whilst I was overseas, Bob asked to sell the book at auction as he had to move to a small retirement flat; the book got £300. I shudder to think of what I had thrown out.

There was to be little surveying as the Estate office was mainly involved in upgrading of canal side domestic properties. Do people take jobs today with such little concept of the reality of what is involved? I had learnt to drive both motorcycles and cars, still exciting in a Leeds of cobbled streets and tram-lines. With little formality I was provided with a Morris Minor from a car pool for outside trips. Many lock and bridge houses were inaccessible by road, so I often spent days walking along canals or hitching lifts on barges. Once I walked my way from Sheffield to the River Trent, noting pipes in and out and overhead wires, called way-leaves as I recall. It took days; maybe they just wanted me out of the office. I set up a works motoring club. I had a huge heavy ex-army motor cycle. I organised treasure hunts and even a dinner dance in Leeds City Hotel. Still under 18, surely I could not have been legally liable for these activities? Maybe it was just that arrogance of youth to do anything.

Older friends used to take me into public houses, although on reflection I was legally too young. I didn't really like bitter anyway but could manage a sweet cider. Pubs were dank, nicotine-stained, smoke-filled, dark brown wood varnished places and seemed rather alien which did not strike me as particularly friendly. I remember one wild and vehemently pursed argument about Japanese goods which were just beginning to come on the market. Anyone who bought such after the treatment meted out to our prisoners of war was a traitor fit only for shooting. I recall one guy wildly screaming. Fortunately we have moved on.

Out of hours near home I arranged the resurfacing and reactivation of a local hard court tennis club, took part in amateur dramatics, and went on weekend retreats, all mainly church-based. Two nights a week I volunteered at the Crypt, a night street shelter for the homeless attached to St George's Church. I did the booking in, served soup and even led unaccompanied evening prayers; "Abide with Me" was a favourite hymn which we sang. These were pre-drug days, but many were addicted to methylated spirits. The Crypt had that pervading nose-tingling smell of disinfectant which had put me off hospitals during father's illness. During day-time the more employable of our night lodgers worked operating jigs making metal coat hangers, then an innovation.

Realizing I was no nearer to becoming the overseas land surveyor I yearned to be, I left for the Ordnance Survey where I had been promised the training I wanted. After a few training months in Chessington, I was posted to Warrington. My work mates sent me to find "digs" to a local well-known brothel on Liverpool Road. The "Madam" interviewed me in a flouncy pink negligee thing whilst sprawled on her huge bed in an over fussy boudoir surrounded by many over-fed cats. Innocently I asked about packed lunches, but she kindly said that she didn't think her place would quite suit me. Next day my work mates roared with laughter when they heard of my visit, I suppose it was a variation on the young lad being sent to the stores for a sky-hook.

Eventually I ended up in a "Coronation Street" style, damp tenement with low watt bulbs and an outside pit latrine. My landlady, unbelievably called Mrs Greed, a name Charles Dickens would have appreciated, certainly lived up to her name! A small can of baked beans lasted for breakfast all week. The front room was never used and kept as a sort of shrine to her presumably war dead husband whose ashes were kept in a jar on the mantle shelf. We "lived" in the back room by an old black range with a tap in the scullery for washing and everything else. Prior to visiting the outside latrine, I was solemnly given a page torn from a pile of comic books she sat on in lieu of a cushion. To ascend the narrow unlit stair case I had to edge up sideways to avoid the sticky dripping walls. My fellow trainee surveyors fared little better. There was a US Air Force base nearby whose staff could afford to pay far more and rent the better places.

I enjoyed the practicality and precise detail of the field surveying work, although heights still troubled me. But whatever the legislation was for the continuing education of youth, the truth was that no one was really interested in investing in any worth-while, long-term training for any one about to do their national service.

My papers, the "Queen's shilling" (as a postal order) and rail warrant came through for me to report to a Pontefract barracks on 6 November 1958 as a conscript in the Yorkshire Brigade.

Chapter 3 - Army service

During my first year of National Service I spent a bleak winter on the North Yorkshire Moors with the Green Howards Regiment, based in Richmond. We conscripts were integrated with both regular recruits and potential Education Corps sergeant instructors. Many of these future teachers were extremely talented, both as musicians and artistes, and we put on a well received rather bawdy Christmas talent show in the barracks theatre. We had decorated the theatre with a liberated Christmas tree we had

carried marching in column over many miles back to camp. I found that I was a good marksman which was both gratifying and enjoyable. I was introduced to Newcastle Brown and in a drunken stupor committed the heinous sin of walking across the hallowed parade square. It had snowed and our boot prints were frozen evidence; all those with Size 10 boots were dragged out of bed. No defence, another military lesson learnt: do what you must but never get caught. In those pre TV days, cinema advertising was the vogue. At over six foot tall, incongruously as a National Service conscript in another unit, I was selected to take part in a recruiting film for the Green Howards, wearing such new equipment that it was to be a decade before I ever saw it, let alone use it, again. It was a happy almost carefree time, decisions were made for us and the Green Howards was a genuinely solicitous family regiment. It was a fine stone-built warm barracks, now converted to a trendy upmarket housing estate.

Later, for no discernable reason, typical of National Service, I was transferred to the Intelligence Corps in Maresfield, Sussex. After six months surveillance and interrogation training, I was given a book and a pack of gramophone records to rise to the dizzy heights of training typists. This was just after the Suez debacle, but when Cyprus was still considered to be a hotbed of undercover terrorist activity. The camp woods were full of grey Soviet artillery pieces and other military hardware brought back from Egypt. To supplement our meagre National Service stipend, we volunteered to take part in weekend practical exercises with regular and territorial soldiers, in what I now realise were rather dubious disorientation interrogation techniques involving water, deprivation of light, confinement and excessive noise. We dressed up in strange foreign uniforms of which there seemed to be an unlimited stock and to us it was rather like amateur dramatics; although in the light of what we all now know, perhaps it was rather more sinister. The thought of spending another year of relative mindless inactivity routinely churning out typists appalled me; so I applied for officer selection. This resulted in my instant ostracism by all, not only my fellow barrack room-mates. With no A levels, I had not been judged potential officer material, but after persistence I got to the three-day selection board. Always the easy confident talker, full of ideas and essentially a pragmatic problem solver, I was accepted for officer training. Surprisingly my choice of land surveyor in the Royal Engineers was accepted, although I never ever became a land surveyor in the proper sense! We endured mindless sweating in Aldershot drilled by, sworn and screamed at by a brain dead Lancashire Fusilier sergeant, perhaps to filter out the faint-hearted. There was the usual scrubbing of floors with toothbrushes, cutting grass with mini scissors and more, all of which I found mildly hilarious. Everyone seemed so intensely serious, yet really all I recall was cycling up to London one evening with a room-mate on his tandem for a "night out". We certainly would have had no spare money, so it must have been just because we were not allowed to do it, and in any event I'd never ridden a tandem before. A few weeks later we Sappers were sent for training to Gillingham near Chatham, home of the Royal Engineers. Sapper officers were referred to as mad, Methodist or married. But to get married then as an officer you had to be over 26 and only then with the permission of your Commanding Officer (CO). Even that was not straightforward. A colleague wanted to marry a divorced woman who in those times was unacceptable and, as he insisted, he was obliged to resign.

After some months of essentially practical and useful training, I "passed out" as an officer and was posted to Northern Germany. A surplus of National Service officers meant we had little to do, so I was sent to the Harz Mountains for ski training - at which I failed miserably, never quite mastering the right turn. To make up numbers I then became a designated bridge player - useful and mentally challenging. Occasionally we had to serve as military guards on the military train that plied daily from West Germany through Soviet occupied East Germany to a divided and still largely bomb shattered, un-reconstructed Berlin. This was a pre-wall Berlin but a decidedly vibrant, alive and exciting city. As military we were allowed free access to a bleak East Berlin. We had to go in uniform and at least in pairs. Our West German currency was worth five times as much in the East. In East Berlin we had free access to the best seats in any theatre and could buy cameras or LP records literally for shillings. The important thing was not to doze off on the tram or U-Bahn and end up in East Germany, definitely out of bounds. The whole boundary arrangement was confusing and seemed surreal.

I tried a spell as a motor cycle trials rider. Bikes were heavy 500cc monsters and took some holding; horses were easier. For a competition on Lüneburg Heath, my unit entered a team of three riders. My petrol fuel tank cap was either loose or the tank overfilled. My crutch was feeling warm and on looking down I found that my riding breeches were on fire. I jumped off the burning bike just before it exploded rather dramatically. My fellow team riders rode past without a glance (they thought my burning bike was a deliberately placed warning to go slower) as the first-aiders were trying to strip off my tight riding breeches and offer me sweet tea for "shock". I wasn't in shock but was livid to be out of the competition! For the next trials, I was not selected for the team.

We seemed to spend an interminable time on part pre-scripted exercises deep in German forests playing at soldiers. As Sappers this meant much bridge building or ferrying troops, vehicles and equipment on rafts across rivers, a practical and real test. On one exercise we had to live inside a new model Armoured Personnel Carrier (APC) during a simulated nuclear attack, for days we were not allowed to go out or open any hatches. Living, heating reconstituted food and eating, working and, yes, even defecating, in such close proximity with four other soldiers was a true bonding exercise. I was very fortunate with my team. It taught us all much tolerance and acceptance of each other's foibles and above all to be tidy with our personal kit. Not all APC teams were so fortunate. It all got much better when I was later to become a skipper on small sailing boats in the Baltic.

In March I was sent to the Advanced Watermanship Training Centre based in Kiel. 'Advanced Watermanship' is Army speak for sailing. An entry qualification was the ability to swim 50 yards in full clothing. I was unable to swim. When growing up, due to the polio scare, all public swimming pools had been closed. I bluffed it, ticked the box on the application entry form certifying myself as a swimmer. As a soldier I would have had to do the test in reality. When the time came for me to actually swim or drown, I found I was a natural swimmer. If you really want something enough and put your mind to it, anything is possible. I was trained to become a coastal skipper on a fleet of small German "prize" 30 square metre four-berth yachts. I think the size referred to the sail area. We used paraffin for lamps and cooking; there was no engine. Our navigation equipment was a chart with a hand-held military compass. I just revelled in it and stayed on all year. Still sailing, or becalmed, I missed my elder brother's wedding which did not enhance my family relationships. I was still sailing around the Danish island of Fyn, when my National Service officially ended; extended by hand-written half-page note from my Colonel CO. I later signed on for nine more years which effectively now confirmed me as a Regular officer.

For this I had to attend a regular commission selection board (RCB) in Warminster before being accepted. Perhaps this was surprising in an army that seemed to be obsessed with family connections. My father had never served in the army during the last war. He had certainly at times driven an ambulance, but was he medically excused military service, from childhood he had always worn spectacles, or was he a pacifist? As an Accountant he was certainly not in any reserved occupation; then you never asked and so you never knew. Grandfather, farming in New Zealand, enlisted to fight in the Boer War, sailing to the Cape complete with his horse, so I made something of this. Passing this RCB meant attending another year's engineering training back in Chatham. As the senior "young" officer I was accorded a number of privileges, and I suppose some responsibilities which do not register so I must have taken them lightly. Our Chief Instructor was the Colonel (CO) with whom I had played bridge and sailed during my time in Germany. He must have seen little merit in my formal training as I spent my year mainly crewing for him on every UK off-shore race. Before my "training" year ended I was sent to Dover as the Junior Leaders' Regiment new sailing officer. These training establishments for youngsters provided potential senior non-commissioned officers from 16 years with military, academic with a heavy emphasis on sports and adventure training; sadly now superseded due to the increased school leaving age. I must admit to never sitting any professional or technical examinations, and had to accept my fellow students' wry comments that I had sailed through my assessment to get my enhanced regular officer "qualification" pay. These times were essentially enjoyable, often irresponsible, but I had learned my lessons the hard way and was rarely caught out.

The Junior Leaders' Regiment had been donated a 12 berth, lumbering, Malayan built, quad-masted boat called "Boleh" - Malaysian for "can do". I was asked to skipper it. This was an unusual vessel which looked like a floating oil rig. It was ideal for energetic youngsters as it took about 16 strong-arm actions to just raise the mainsail. To skipper this I had to pass a practical Offshore Skipper examination. My very elderly civilian examiner came on board, said "go to Alderney" and promptly went into his bunk where he remained asleep until we docked. Alderney is not the easiest harbour for a novice to enter as you sail up to some high cliffs until, at the very last moment, two points are aligned when you turn sharply 90 degrees starboard (right). I passed and, with miserable night vision, was relieved to have made landfall in daylight and on a slack tide.

Sailing up and down the busy channel with only a compass, parallel rule, tide tables and chart was true navigation. Generally my first mate was a grizzled retired marine working in the Regiment as a physical training instructor, the original quiet silent type, but to me a veritable rock. Just off Dover we once passed some wreckage and a couple of face down floating bodies. I was for stopping but, accompanied by a more senior officer as passenger, I was overruled *"for the good of our young soldiers"*. I noted their position but, with no radios, was unable to notify the Coast Guards until we returned three days later. This was shortly after the Great Train Robbery whose gang it was rumoured had left Ramsgate in a motor cruiser which had blown up. I'll never know if these two bodies had their pockets stuffed with fivers. Once, caught in a storm off Cherbourg, we lost our dinghy and most of our sails and some rigging and were forced to call into port to make some repairs. With little money and no decent or dry clothes I was obliged to visit the local British Consular Officer for a loan to repair our boat and buy other necessities. Walking or rather squelching down his long carpeted office, I proffered my soggy ID card and the photograph fell off. Grovelling on the floor under his desk to retrieve my photograph was probably not the most auspicious way to start what was to be a difficult interview. I got the loan.

Boleh had a platform low down at the stern with a hole that served as a latrine, it was out of the way, very practical and comfortable. Roy my first mate used to spend hours down there reading a newspaper. Boleh was a big boat and we generally had to moor far out. One quiet Sunday morning in Alderney harbour Roy was in his usual position. With the tide going out his backside was exposed only out to sea - but eventually the tide turned and the boat swung round so that our stern was, well you can imagine it.

Most term-time afternoons were devoted to a wide range of sporting activities: horse riding, fencing, canoeing, water polo or more. If these youngsters were good at anything it was generally nurtured and developed. I arranged the first mass cross channel canoe crossing and piloted the support launch which the canoes followed. French Customs were a little bemused but cooperative. We returned the following day and UK Customs were less cooperative. Quite what they thought these tired youngsters could conceal in their two man canoes was a mystery. But then these were the same customs who, when Bleriot landed on the white cliffs of Dover in July 1909, had kept him waiting for hours for clearance. His flight took 37 minutes and customs clearance over four hours, so some things never change! The Dover customs officers log book noted that this arrival was most inconvenient, but they did not consider the arrival of air machines would become a regular occurrence. On rainy afternoons I would arrange free entry to the matinee shows in the local cinema. Thirty boisterous, fit, young 16 year-olds in a cinema could get a little wild together. The manager requested they should sit dispersed amongst the other customers, generally pensioners attending the cheaper matinees. Not always a good idea. During both the "Zulu" and "D-Day" films there is a military roll call. I cringed as I heard my group, dotted around the cinema, answering their names with a sharp "Sir!" during the roll call.

In the forces you get to do many things. It is a cheap source of readily mobilized labour with its own backup logistics. We carried out searches over wild terrain for lost children; we acted as extras in the film "Those Magnificent Men in Their Flying Machines"; and we provided buglers and a horse for the 400th centenary celebrations of Shakespeare's birth, a nightly event held over some weeks in Dover Castle. I'm not sure how that responsibility fell to me as I didn't ride well and was certainly no musician. The performance, composed of popular excerpts from Shakespeare's plays started just before dusk with our buglers sounding a fanfare on the battlements as the sun set over the sea. The horse appeared later in Richard III's "kingdom for a horse" speech. In darkness I led the horse onto the lush grass stage with the ruined battlements as a backdrop, and then crept or stumbled away. Cue floodlights, excitable horse reared dramatically, actor King Richard, valiantly clinging on, made speech. Horse and King exit stage right. After the closing fanfare, I took the horse back to our barracks on an adjacent hill on the other side of town. I normally led the horse but maybe this time I was late for something or perhaps the horse was less skittish than usual; in any event I decided to ride back. Unknown to me there are a whole set of traffic regulations for riding a horse on a public highway, particularly at night. Ignorance of the law is no defence and riding a horse without lights was a road traffic offence. Another blot on my record and many extra duties, but I made a great friend of the local Police Inspector who was far more relaxed about it all than our rather humourless career-conscious Adjutant.

The hidden potential and ability of our young soldiers knew few bounds. In addition to arranging one of the first mass cross Channel crossings with a team of over ten two-man canoes, I coached a winning team of canoeists to get top places in the Devizes to Westminster canoe race. Morgan was one of the first youngsters to reach Gold standard on the new Duke of Edinburgh's Award scheme which he proudly collected personally from the Duke at the Palace. With commitment, time and training there seemed to be nothing that could not be achieved if they set their minds to it.

During the last week of term (this regiment operated on a three academic term basis) we were allowed, within reason, to do some practical out of barracks "character building" exercises. My aunt had recently returned from overseas and was determined to build her own house and needed some tree stumps clearing from the site. It was a few hours away and seemed an ideal project. We had cleared most of the stumps with small charges of explosive when I returned to camp for some duty, leaving my Sergeant to remove the last two stumps. Any unused explosives had to fully accounted and returned to the ammunition dump, which was a lengthy and bureaucratic procedure. My Sergeant decided to "save time" and packed the remaining explosive into these last two stumps. This house site was bounded by two busy roads; one stump flew across one road and straight through the roof of a house which had won a 1950s Ideal Home award. We never traced the other stump. Certain roof reparations were needed, all good practical tradesman activity! Only later I realized that this site was over the Sevenoaks railway tunnel, but the trains had kept running. My aunt became a close friend of this neighbour whose house roof we had inadvertently bombarded; so I suppose it served as some sort of an introduction. I'm not sure how many rules I'd broken, but with my current record I could not expect much leniency. I began to look for some posting a little less constraining. Fellow officer and accomplished self publicist Blashford-Snell, whose inspiration went on to found Operations Drake and Raleigh, apparently could do no wrong. Whilst he blew up local goldfish ponds, or abandoned bootless young soldiers on Dartmoor to find their own way back to camp, he received much media acclaim.

Most of our young recruits, the future potential non-commissioned officers, were from broken homes, or generally un-cared for and unloved. When not sailing, during the long summer holidays, few of these trainees seemed to have much desire to return to unwelcoming homes. I took small groups of them through France to Spain, Italy and Switzerland in a Nuffield donated minibus, often towing a small Enterprise sailing dinghy.

On my first trip I learnt that ten young lads bursting with energy, fitness and intelligence, when freed from the constraints of barracks discipline, could run circles round me, so on subsequent trips I took a Sergeant with me. With army tinned ration packs, tents and concessionary fuel, we were able to do three to four week camping trips for minimal amounts of money. In the early sixties continental travel was still quite a novelty.

I'd begun to realise that perhaps I was not quite in the mould of other career regular officers who seemed so deadly earnest about everything and unquestioning of every petty order. I certainly did not consider myself a rebel and I tried hard to give at least the appearance of conforming. Yet I constantly seemed to be at odds with my superiors in Dover, so I applied to go to the newly independent Kenya as a seconded Training Officer.

Before being accepted for secondment (a sort of attachment) I had to be interviewed by the elderly General Officer Commanding Home Division based in London's Chelsea Barracks. He was straight out of "Oh! What a Lovely War" and advised me that *"black chaps [were] not quite like us"*. Earlier I'd attended a long signals instructors' course in Chatham and, as the only officer, had been partnered with a Nepalese Gurkha. This improved my Morse speed, sending and receiving incredibly. Soldiers often used Morse code to have clandestine private conversations that officers could not decipher. I learnt how to improvise an aerial and how even a barbed wire fence could be an effective antenna. I was determined to miss nothing and be as good as if not better than anyone else. I found this a fascinating course, although I'm unsure what use the army skills at fault finding on valve radios are now. I passed with the only A grade, practical and verbal tests again, not written. From my Ordnance Survey time, I'd trained with Sudanese, Ghanaians and Nigerians. In Dover my Sergeant was Fijian and my driver Jamaican. Those I had taught were from as many countries with as many religions. I have never felt there was a "them and us".

Much later I was to attend a "racial awareness" course sponsored by Voluntary Services Overseas (VSO), run in Sheffield Hallam University by earnest drab women who insisted that we all harboured deep seated hidden racial prejudices. I do not agree and found the General's comment on "black chaps" ill informed and unnecessary.

During the holidays, as I was preparing to go to Kenya, I returned to collect my vaccination and other papers from the Dover barracks. The medical centre had mistakenly posted them to Kenya. I was flying in a few days and needed them, so they gave me another set of vaccinations with a new set of papers. The resulting double dose of vaccinations caused me to sleep for two days!

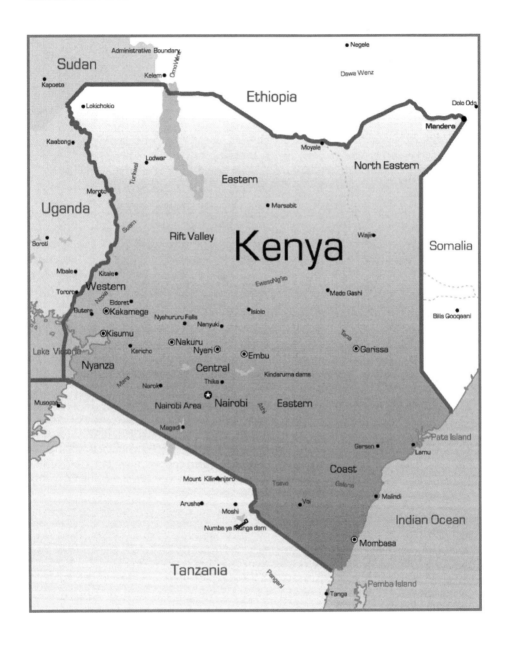

Chapter 4 - Kenya

My flight out to Kenya was on a BOAC Comet, one of the first civilian aircraft used by the military. We landed at Nairobi Airport, not the RAF Embakasi military airport previously used, and I was not met. I had no visa and was promptly put in the deportees lounge where I stayed for some uncomfortable hours until found by an embarrassed Air Force Movements clerk. The air was warm and balmy with the heady evening scent of flowers and the loud clicking of cicadas . Somehow it just made everything seem right. I knew I'd manage here and was determined "to make it work".

My first task in Kenya as a relatively young, recently promoted Captain, was to remove some racially derogatory graffiti left by a departing British Army from a latrine block. So much for my anticipated added responsibilities! After a poor start trying to train engineers selected from the largely illiterate and innumerate loyal fighting veterans from the Kings African Rifles (KAR), I searched old KAR educational records to select better potential recruits. Intriguingly my attention was drawn to a Ugandan soldier. Before independence the Kenyan, Ugandan and Tanganyikan armies were under one central command structure and their records were still held centrally in Kenya. Despite constantly failing his promotion exams to become a sergeant, he was recommended to pass as he was a "very useful boxer". That Sergeant was later to become President Idi Amin of Uganda, notorious for corruption, human rights abuses, ethnic persecution and extra judicial killings. The number of people killed as a result of his brutal regime is estimated to be between 100,000 and 500,000.

We later enlisted our craftsmen recruits directly from missionary technical and vocational schools. They were young, disciplined and technically well trained. Within a year we had built up an effective, reasonably well-equipped, construction unit, initially building bridges and roads in the National Parks which provided us with free construction materials. We helped open up to the public Lake Nakuru as a National Park, with its millions of pink flamingos. In the Aberdare Park we worked with the knowledgeable Warden, Bill Woodley, at the time of the filming of "Born Free" in 1965 and I helped feed the many orphaned lion cubs used in the filming. Whilst in the Aberdares I was invited out hunting in the Rift Valley below, all I had was the standard military issue .303 rifle but managed to shoot a dik-dik in the afternoon which impressed my companions and provided our supper. A dik-dik is a very small deer that I later learnt mated for life. From pre-dawn the next morning we crept downwind for ages in the increasingly searing heat and finally shot an Eland in an unsuspecting grazing herd. It was wounded and we followed its blood trail for miles through hot inhospitable acacia scrub before it finally collapsed. We took it back to camp and fed all our soldiers. Kenyans love eating meat. However good a marksman I was, there was something deeply disturbing about killing animals and I never went hunting again.

Much later I was to meet George Adamson whose actions inspired this film, but sadly, as so many dedicated conservationists before and after him, he was locally misunderstood and murdered. In the early independence of the mid sixties, Kenya seemed to be a very popular location, particularly with US film companies. There were many film units shooting instantly forgettable films, most of which I never saw as they were not screened locally. They seemed very wasteful with their resources and when they left we used their discarded set materials, wire, timber and hessian, for our own construction work. As a unit we had already built up a good reputation and were increasingly being deployed on "hearts and minds" tasks, such as civilian flood relief and even an early school reconstruction at Ahero near the malarial Port Victoria in the west - a portent of things to come for me when four decades later I found myself building schools in Ethiopia. For a reason that now puzzles me, I travelled alone on a public bus to Port Victoria to join my soldiers already deployed there. Whoever said that to understand any country you need to travel on its public transport is absolutely correct and most of these trips are rich in memories. In those early days of independence Kenyans still had to carry a kipande, an ID card with their thumb print on. I am not sure whether it's a requirement now. That these buses are full of livestock is well known - the lady by the window seat next to me had a noisy cockerel under her skirts. At one call of nature break, then referred to as a "wet", I returned to find the lady sprawled over my seat with the cockerel protesting loudly, she had died. African's attitude to and reaction to death continues to confuse me. As soon as I think I am beginning to comprehend it, I am thrown by something new. Here in Western Kenya they seemed to be essentially quick and practical. Her thumb was cut off and with her ID handed to the police. Her body was given to someone, I assume for burial, with her bag and the cockerel, maybe in payment? The driver had a schedule to keep and we seemed to be on our way in a very short time. It was to be a long time before I went on another public bus, in fact not until Indonesia. On arrival at Port Victoria the village chief gave me his best hut, yet I was so consumed by mosquitoes that the next morning I thought I was blind as my face had puffed up so much. That I have never contracted malaria, then or in life-time overseas in malarial areas (with colleagues and friends literally falling down around me), is a testament to whatever the army made us take daily with our rations. To get malaria was, in army parlance, a chargeable offence; failing to take the pill and making yourself "unfit for duty" was not acceptable. Certainly, ever since I've always been a disciplined pill taker when under doctor's orders.

Soon we were building camps, roads and airfields in operational areas along the Kenya borders with Ethiopia and Somalia to the north and east. My British Major was ever critical; I was becoming too "troppo" (native) in fraternising with the locals. Yet I was working, living and sleeping with Kenyan officers, some of them new Makerere University graduates, all the cream and intelligentsia of this newly independent country. I was the only expatriate living in the Gilgil barracks and certainly the only one in the field. Was I to become a Trappist monk?

I moved out of the barracks to a guest house in the Nakuru Show ground, but listening continuously to a week of Bert Kaempfert's Swinging Safari during the Annual Agricultural Show was more than I could take. This was a time when many expatriates were fleeing Kenya, uncertain what independence would bring, so I found it was easy to rent a three acre abandoned plot outside Nakuru with a small, fully furnished bungalow for £15 a month. The hot water system was a 40 gallon oil drum set on an outside open barbecue style fire. I once came back from weeks in the field, on safari, to find the plot being cultivated by squatters. They were gently moved on by the police with profuse apologies. A recent political speech by Kenyatta saying that all land was now free had been misunderstood; they explained. I encouraged my Abaluyha house staff, despite their age, still regrettably referred to as "shamba boys", to start planting the whole plot for themselves.

My store keeper requested home leave as he claimed his daughter had been bewitched. On returning from this leave he said he'd been unable to counter the curse and requested compassionate leave later when he had saved more money to buy the necessary pure white sheep as a sacrifice. Only the Major could authorise this and he refused. I was criticised for giving any credence to this "local nonsense". The daughter died and the storeman got his leave, to bury her. We had an Irish medical officer, Brendan O'Duffy, who liked his whiskey and of whom it was irreverently said his patients got anaesthetized by his breathing on them. A few years later in a Nairobi club he was relating a recent post mortem he had conducted. A young soldier had died on a football field after being struck on the head by a football, yet he could find nothing medically wrong with him. He called it parasympathetic rebound: fright to you and me. It was the same storeman; his wife having previously died; had they all really been cursed? I began to have a grudging respect for local beliefs which presaged many similar incidents throughout my life, not all of them overseas.

I continued to be chastised to "maintain standards", or be repatriated, but it was the Major who went home early, it was said with bilharzia. At the bottom of the Major's garden, his gardener was performing witch doctor rituals, no fairies there then. He was the first of very few bosses I struggled to respect. But bad times often lead to better and his replacement was a joy. An army pilot, an experienced Korean battle veteran and part of the Ghanaian UN peace keeping force in the Congo; he was full of quiet wisdom, immeasurable African wisdom and gentle kindness. Dear Don Wright, my hero, I was both happy and proud to remain his life-long friend.

Driving up a wet slippery winding laterite road into the Aberdare National Park, a black cat crossed in front of us. My driver stopped dead and resolutely refused to drive any further. Black cats might be lucky for us, but not so here. *"Bad luck"* he said and no amount of persuasion would change his mind. We returned to camp and later I heard that a tree had fallen and blocked the road. Laterite (a sort of red earth) roads are never easy after rain and we were called to remove a crashed timber lorry which had driven or slid into a railway bridge abutment. As we pulled the smashed lorry back and out with our recovery crane the driver's severed head rolled out of the crushed cab windscreen. It seemed to bounce for ever down the road until it lodged in some acacia bushes by the verge. The British Warrant Officer operating the recovery crane, a purported Korean veteran (well he wore the campaign medals), promptly threw up. Amazingly this was his first dead body; perhaps he stayed with the reserves in the rear. I had met a Major who served actively throughout the Second World War and vowed he had never taken his pistol out of its holster, let alone fire it.

I spent most of my time "on safari" with troops who spoke little English. I soon picked up the lingua franca - Swahili - rather in the way a child learns. When visiting the Nairobi Army HQ, I took the practical conversational language test and passed at a good enough mark to get extra pay.

My Kenya tour was three years and there was no provision for inter tour home leave during this time as I suppose flights then were relatively expensive. We got good holidays and I was able to visit most of the Kenyan National Parks which were fast being developed. The roads were not good and I lost more than one windscreen due to flying stones, but I took the precaution of having a pair of motor cycling goggles with me. I had the added bonus of being given a free pass to all parks for the work we had done for the Parks. Tourism in Kenya was not so developed at that time, unlike in Uganda which was a much more popular destination. I also was given a free pass to the luxurious Mount Kenya Safari Lodge in Nanyuki, founded by US film star William Holden and others in 1959, for an airstrip we had built for them. Called by the locals Mount Kirinyaga the colonial settlers must have found that word too difficult and abbreviated it to Mount Kenya. Jomo Kenyatta, the first President of the newly independent Republic of Kenya was christened Johnson (a Mission School given name) but changed his name to Jomo Kenyatta (person of Kenya) whilst studing in the UK in the 1920's. Originally both Mount Kenya and the higher but easier to climb Kilimanjaro were in British East Africa, but Kaiser Wilhelm II complained to his grandmother Queen Victoria that she had two East African mountains and he had none. Kilimanjaro was then "given" to German East Africa and the map re-drawn, so arbitrary were colonial boundaries fixed, nothing thought of the Masai people who lived astride the boundary.

In those carefree, heady days we drove to Uganda for long weekends, there were no borders or border guards. The only indication of crossing a border was that portraits hanging in the public bars and hotels were of a different president. The Nairobi Club, with an active, new, majority Kenyan middle-class membership kept Queen Elizabeth II of England's portrait up for at least twenty years following independence. Were these lingering longings for a colonial era? I made longer trips to Tanganyika, later to become Tanzania on its union with Zanzibar. President Nyerere's motorcades were impressive. Appropriately, as a man of the people, they all drove in Volkswagens. Throughout the old Federation of East Africa, the police were still smart, courteous, helpful and uncorrupt.

Running slow, grinding, long military supply convoys along sandy, barely marked tracks to the Somali border region was no adventure. Sinking in wadis was an ever present danger, but ambushes and undetectable plastic land mines slowed our progress and added to the uncertainty. Our vehicles, mainly requisitioned public works department and painted bright orange yellow, were stripped of doors and glass, our only anti-mine measure. Although we had Kenyan Army infantry escorts it was unwise to relax our vigilance. Our escorts could be brutal with any suspects, often with any one they saw. Shoot first then check for Identity. If they were found to have ID cards, these were burnt and their livestock confiscated. Armies don't change, they are trained to fight, indeed kill; days and weeks of boring inactivity can make them itch for a scrap at the slightest excuse. During one particularly well staged ambush, usually prefaced by blown culverts or well placed land mines, our accompanying Kenyan padre stood up, screaming hysterically *"Don't shoot, don't shoot, I'm a man of God"* - our concealed position was now compromised. This situation was later repeated with fatal results when an Italian Priest was foolishly collecting his mail outside the Freetown Central Post Office during a coup attempt. Faith whilst important; should always be tempered with common sense; it is no bullet proof vest.

After a few months I was the only member of our small expatriate training team left in the field. The others found it difficult or their wives complained. In Mandera on the Somalia Ethiopia borders I built myself a corrugated iron shed and parked my personal one ton tipper truck in front of it; tippers have strong sides. We had no smaller vehicles, not good for land mines. Our camp was regularly mortared at nights, but I preferred to get a reasonable night's sleep and rarely went, as advised, to the trenches. One morning I woke up to find my chicken tied to my bed frame – shot by a stray bullet, a little too close to my mattress and unnerving. We were in camp with our escort Infantry company which provided day-time security in our quarry, the road and the airfield. We worked the full 12 hours of daylight every day; the infantry in six hour shifts. Our labourers were Somali detainees, effectively prisoners. They were paid a shilling a day by the District

Commissioner and also got some tea leaves and a bit of food, which included a can of sardines – although Somalis do not eat fish. Unknowingly this was my first experience of "food for work".

Kenya was reputedly the place of Happy Valley where colonial settlers' wife swopping seemed more the rule than the exception. Some of this behaviour must have permeated in the new indigenous Kenyan army and I remember a strong lecture given by the Army Commander Brigadier Ndola where he rambled on for long before finally stating most empathetically that this *"jumping on fellow officers wives must stop"*. It was difficult to keep a straight face. I remember another badly received lecture we had from some well meaning lady from the US on birth control, not a subject that had much resonance with the average Kenyan male. One soldier said he had a better method than that she was expounding, *"Ha"*, she said *"and how many children does your wife have"*. *"Three"* he answered truthfully. *"so what is your better method?"* she asked disdainfully. *"Well I sleep with other women"* he replied, so obvious to him. That soldier was my driver Thomas Muindi Mulwa. So much for birth control Kenyan style.

The Kenyan Infantry Major sent a message for me to spare some men to help pump water for the camp from a water hole in the river as he needed to drill his men for an upcoming parade. Unwisely I replied verbally that my men were too busy. This was insubordination in an operational area, serious and shameful. Marching bent near double into the CO's small tent under escort was not very dignified. My captain formal escort was Marsden Madoka, who went on to become the President's Aide de Camp (ADC) and to marry his daughter. He is now a successful farmer, business man and cabinet minister. These men were the future of Kenya. To refuse was so wrong, so foolish and quite inexcusable, but being confined to barracks with many extra duties was hardly much of a punishment when, in any event, there was nowhere else to go.

In our Officer's mess tent we played Monopoly, continuously for months. Monopoly money became real money. We had no use for Kenyan shillings where we were; there were no shops and nothing to buy. When you left for work or duty you took your Monopoly money with you. The District Commissioner, an ex-missionary, Oxford educated, local man was an honorary mess member but wisely did not play. Two of his bright new District Officers were posted here, joined the mess and started to play. We all assumed someone else had explained the rules, our mess rules that is. By omission they were unaware that the Major commanding was never allowed to lose. One memorable occasion after losing to these two upstarts, this tough battle scarred major stood up. Incandescent with rage, he berated them for cheating. So angry, puffing in and out, he banned them forever from "his" mess, and in his fury his kikoi (a wrap round skirt-like material) fell down. We all nearly choked with suppressed mirth. He was a fantastic, much respected Major, fearless in the field and a brave fighter, real old school KAR. But like so many of the best active commanders, to be in barracks does not always bring out their best qualities. Mandera was like a foreign legion outpost. During the Second World War it had been garrisoned by the British as an outpost against a possible Italian invasion from Abyssinia, a mile across a seasonal river which was the border. A number of British officers found the solitary life unbearable and shot themselves. An Army psychiatrist was posted to assess the situation; and after a few weeks, he too shot himself. The British abandoned the post; in any event the Italians surrendered in 1943.

Building airfields I learnt how to fly small single-engine planes and got my Private Pilot's Licence. With my eyesight I was told I would never qualify. If I'm ever told it's impossible, I will always make that extra effort to prove some one wrong. If you really want anything, go for it and you'll achieve it. Stuck with my poor colour perception, I was unable to upgrade this to a commercial licence which was disappointing. Flying was freedom and exhilarating, if at times heart stopping when sucked up and down by the strong Rift Valley thermals. I sometimes begged lifts with new Kenyan Air Force pilots. I knew they'd try to terrify me but it was a price I was prepared to pay. I was told of an early trainee pilot who had crash landed just after take-off - with no fuel. Infamously he had assured his instructor his fuel gauge had read "E" - for enough. "F" he said was surely for "finished". F for him was also fail. Passing practical examinations or interviews, or even learning lengthy poems or parts in amateur dramatics, I could manage. I positively revelled in this and had few nerves, but put me in room for a written exam, however well prepared I thought I was, and my mind became blank.

Post-independence Kenya was still a rather wild irreverent place. Sports clubs and amateur dramatics played a big part in a still essentially brash, privileged, colonialist life-style amongst settlers and expatriates. Their still assumed superiority made me feel distinctly uncomfortable. Stories abounded of dealing with recalcitrant local staff who stole and how smart the colonialists thought they were. I was once proudly presented by an applicant for cook with a much folded greasily stained recommendation letter. The letter wished his other house work was not as light fingered as his pastry was. Alcohol bottles weren't only marked but marked when inverted to check levels for pilfering. I approved of the story of the settler who, convinced that his staff were drinking the sherry he rarely touched, urinated in the decanter to keep the level steady as he had marked. When the decanter was finally empty and the cook requested another bottle, the settler smugly said well he'd never drunk any and asked where had it all gone? *"Every night in your soup"* the cook replied. Could this be true? Later I read a similar story from Sierra Leone where, in the 1800s, the Bunce Island slaving station commander lost his long awaited and recently delivered new tricorne hat. It had blown away whilst on the river; the oarsman thrown in to retrieve it, a non swimmer, drowned. Annoyed beyond reason the station commander had urinated in the evening rum ration cask. His staff mutinied and murdered him, not so much for the death of the drowned boy but as spoiling their rum ration. His lone unmarked grave stone still stands on Bunce Island, plain stone as his family refused to pay for any engraving, shamed by his deed.

I visited Rhodesia which had recently unilaterally declared independence. It still seemed very much a white colony. Whilst there was no official apartheid, it operated more through an inability of the local Rhodesians to be able to afford to go into those hotels, restaurants and clubs frequented by the colonialists. More of a price bar in effect. Later in South Africa I visited an ex-army friend who was working there as an Engineer. He suggested I should take a job there, as this was the future of Africa. Again I felt distinctly uncomfortable with the strictly enforced apartheid regime and assumed white superiority. It was only after a time there that I realized that "Nur fur blankes" meant reserved for whites, I thought it was "not for whites". I made a donation in a bucket to the "Free Peter Hain" campaign and left. If I'd stayed there I think I too may have been arrested for my distinctly anti-apartheid views.

The Kenyans I worked with were bright and vibrant; they were keen to learn and unafraid of hard work. In the mid sixties the military was the only place that was genuinely integrated with white Kenyans and even a Sikh officer; in truth I felt more comfortable there. I had loved training these young disciplined recruits who were so determined and quick to learn; many of whom later went on to key senior positions. I got a terrific kick out of them going ahead independently, surpassing my knowledge, to plan and build camps, roads, hospitals and more. They were becoming self-sufficient, we had trained the trainers and it was time for me to move on. It had been so fulfilling to do something practical and useful. In Kenya I had lost more than my heart to Africa.

My parent's wedding - 1931

With my brother and sister - 1951

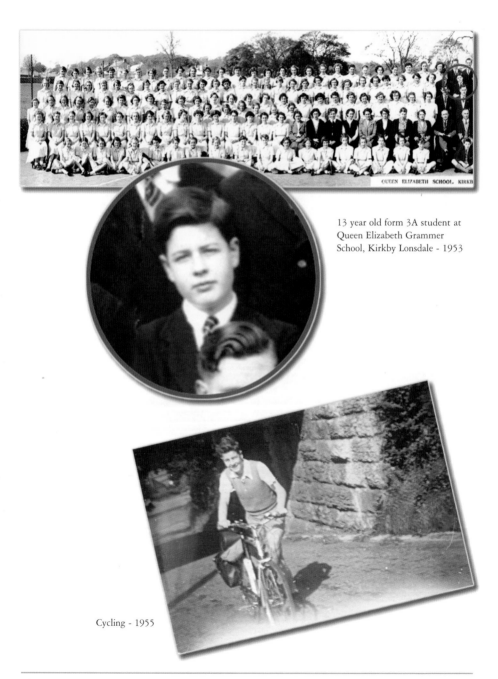

13 year old form 3A student at
Queen Elizabeth Grammer
School, Kirkby Lonsdale - 1953

Cycling - 1955

Royal Hotel, Ventnor

With mother and family about
to tour Europe

Newly commissioned - 1959

In BAOR (Germany)
- 1960

Old style mobile
command centre

APC command post - 1962

Berlin - pre wall - 1960

Sailing - 1961

Alderney harbour light - 1962

Sailing on 'Boleh' English Channel - 1963

Chapter 5 - A Zambian interlude

The thought of returning to Europe into a mechanised hierarchal British Army on the Rhine, still gripped in cold war madness, was not appealing. At that stage of my career I would have been engaged on administration, never my favourite occupation. I preferred to be with and amongst people. The thought of sitting in sterile, windowless strong rooms updating highly classified mine field maps and emergency deployment plans

was not my idea of a life. In Kenya I'd had virtual autonomy way beyond what my rank would have allowed in the British Army. I had been overseeing the practical building of real and tangible construction work that was useful and needed.

There was a vacancy in Zambia; a country presided over by Kenneth Kaunda since their 1964 independence. He professed humanism, although I failed to see the humanism in smashing up a shop whose owner was not a party member, or refusing entry into the ubiquitous public minibus without first showing your political party card.

It took four days to drive my aging Renault from Kenya, picking up a bad bout of debilitating dysentery on the way. Renaults, together with Volkswagens, were great cars for Africa; neither had fan belts, always a drawback when fording deep water. In Tanzania it was the rainy season and I was ploughing successfully through a long flooded section of road, passing many stuck and abandoned vehicles littering the verges. In any seemingly empty stretch of bush in Africa, if you stop or there is any incident, people will appear as if by magic. Many "helpers" came to push me, a service I didn't need. Ever resourceful the "helpers" started pushing me backwards and sideways until we had negotiated an agreed fee. I delight in and can't help but admire the opportunism of Africans. Find a pothole, stand by it, then start filling it in for a passing big car, for coppers, or, making it a bigger pothole, so that any passing car gets stuck, then help them out, for some money of course. I wondered if only this energy, initiative and resourcefulness could be better harnessed and more positively directed. Building the Tanzam (now Tazara) railway were hundreds of glum-faced, drab uniformed Chinese, all accompanied by a constraining political agent; fraternisation was not encouraged. It is much different now with their relative openness, smiles, incessant loud chattering, and latest fashions of the many thousands of Chinese in Africa of today. Perhaps their overt friendliness with the local street girls of the night may not be too welcomed. I can not but wonder if the Chinese will ever leave Africa as they drift away from their contracts and set up their businesses. Are these the new African colonialists?

I had arranged to send my dog, "Zimba", to Zambia by air, but mistakenly it overflew to South Africa. Rhodesia had unilaterally declared independence "UDI". The overland borders were officially and effectively closed, as much as any porous Africa border can claim to be closed. The British Navy was blockading ports of oil and goods for Rhodesia. With closed borders it took some lengthy negotiating to eventually collect Zimba from over the Victoria Falls Bridge. She was brought over to me on a lead by a smart white Rhodesian policeman in his crisp starched khakis; we met half way across the bridge. When Zimba got excited her whole back side shook and she sprayed pee, rather like the larger hippo. When she saw me in the distance she got excited; the policeman never flinched. It seemed reminiscent of some filmed cold war spy exchange, except I had nothing to exchange.

Closed borders meant basic shortages of many goods normally shipped from South Africa. To buy soap, salt, tea or other basics, not only did you have to show your party card but also your fingers were painted with indelible ink to prevent your returning to buy any more of that item that week. A finger was specified for each item. By some unexplained logic, Zambia was supporting the fledgling new state of Biafra which was involved in some appalling conflict whilst attempting to secede from Nigeria. To get a Zambian driving licence there was an obligatory extra fee to be paid ostensibly into the "Biafra fund". There were many Biafran doctors working in Zambia and I vaguely wondered if they would not have been better employed during the civil war disaster in their own country.

Officially I was in Zambia as a "Training Officer", although increasingly this job description was becoming a euphemism for something rather more sinister. Early on in my tour of duty there was some big political rally being held in the bush, much the style of the time. Now five star luxury hotels are preferred. All participants, including the President, were living in a huge tented city. The President's kerosene refrigerator was not working and, as an "Engineer", I was sent for. Never an essentially practical person and often lacking that ability to easily bang a nail in a wall to hang up a picture, I had no time to even be nervous. There were no walls to hide behind in a tented city so everyone knew everyone else's business. I knew the trick of how to get a much travelled kerosene fridge working: upend it for a time to let any gas vacuums settle. It worked, I was vindicated. I was driving a Kenyan registered car, I was wearing an un-badged uniform and I was seen in, and coming out of, the President's tent. Later I realized that I was thought to be one of Kaunda's many undercover agents or spies. They were wrong, but I seemed to make few friends in Zambia.

Was this why I was sent to the far North West of the country to set up and run boat patrols along the River Zambezi border with what was Portuguese Angola? Colonially drawn African borders are neither respected nor observed. The river patrol's principal mission was ostensibly to prevent the colonial occupying Portuguese military entering Zambia in pursuit of Chinese-backed Angolan freedom fighters. We were surely only a token presence. Our patrols were not interested in cross border trade or smuggling, or indeed freedom fighters or terrorists. Any military patrol or, indeed, perceived government presence in any form, is generally unwelcome in Africa, a border patrol even less so. In any event traders, smugglers or fighters all melted into the background and I could find no identifiable group to brief as to our presence. So no one can have told anyone why we were there. Being led by a white perceived "mercenary" was worse still, and our patrol must have been seen as an unwelcome intrusion and a threat to all. In practice everyone was our "enemy".

A thin metal open assault boat is quite indefensible. It has no protection from any helicopter gun ship, and overhanging mangrove swamps are no proof against bullets. As a pawn in another's conflict I was dangerously near to becoming another forgotten statistic. Wars are no solution. Those who supply weaponry are inherently evil, but I have no solution. I make no apology to repeat that, from time immemorial, in any war or conflict zone, it is always the innocent and defenceless who invariably suffer most. It was forty years ago when I was in Zambia and it is still happening now in too many African countries.

My boat patrol crew were all young, bright, intelligent and well educated volunteers. Undoubtedly they must have been attracted by the extra active duty pay. African borders can be unsettling places and even before we arrived the river was full of bodies in eddying pools, decaying African bodies lose colour in patches; it is not a pleasant sight. Soon and increasingly we had too many lingering deaths; shot, burnt or drowned, not always explainable. At least we brought all our soldiers' bodies back to their homes. Something I was to get accustomed to but never could accept: too many empty beds in the mornings. Emotional visits to morgues, stirred up by ranting priests, too many distraught family and ululating mothers who often leapt into open graves hugging their sons' coffins. I attended too many military funerals and coroners' inquests. The carelessness and lack of respect for their dead bodies disturbed me. Faces stuck to deep freeze mortuary sides, as the body filing drawers were pulled open, skin was ripped off. What could I say to these wailing devastated mothers? Beyond platitudes I could neither justify nor explain why their sons had had to die so horribly and so unnecessarily. I was little comfort.

One weekend I drove over the border to Lubumbashi, previously Elizabethville, in the Congo Republic. The city still had the style and grandeur of most ex-French colonies, although now a little scorched, battle scarred and run down. It still boasted grand parks and superb cafés with excellent freshly imported French food, cheeses and pastries, and that alone was well worth the visit. The border guards had the old sterling sub machine gun or Sten gun. When I was waved through the barrier the exchange rate was two large bottles of beer for one Sten gun. I bought them the beer, but declined to take their guns.

After yet another military funeral I'd had enough. I admit to resigning before completing my contract, for the first and only time in my life. I walked out, sold my car for cash and spent some days mingling with tour groups enjoying the pleasures of the Victoria Falls whilst arranging my papers. There were some hefty financial penalties for me I was anxious to avoid, so in effect I left quietly and got on a plane from a small provincial airfield back to Kenya.

I was on my way for an interview I'd arranged with Dottore Franco, Managing Director of the family-run Italian industrial gas manufacturing organization who had a managerial job in West Africa. I thought it was to be in Nigeria, which had just declared some sort of peace after defeating Biafra, but in the event it turned out to be Sierra Leone. I had few preferences and was not fussy. Getting suitable civilian employment with few formal qualifications after a military career was not easy. UK-based companies seemed little interested in employing an ex-military engineer officer from Africa. Integrity and organizational ability in the military were then neither recognised nor appreciated. Thankfully it is quite different now with military and civilian skills far better integrated.

On my way to my interview I picked up a short do-it-yourself style US paper back in the airport entitled something like "Bluff your way in Management". I read it on the plane, picked up the jargon and sailed through my interview. It was early summer in Turin. I remember the blossom, the pasta and wonderful coffee as I spent a few weeks learning the business and basic Italian. After Zambia, this clean orderliness, smartness, my Italian bosses chauffeur's immaculate suit, and exquisite delightful food, was such a wonderful relaxing tonic - but it was not to remain so for long as I boarded the UTA Paris flight for Freetown.

With Bill and Ruth Woodley, Warden,
Aberdare National Park - 1965

One of the "Born Free" cubs,
Mweiga - 1965

Aberdare National Park - 1965

Bungalow at Lanet, near Nakuru - 1965

Kenya Army Engineers
Dress Uniform - 1965

Eating roast "dik dik", my first kill
with driver Muindi Mulwa

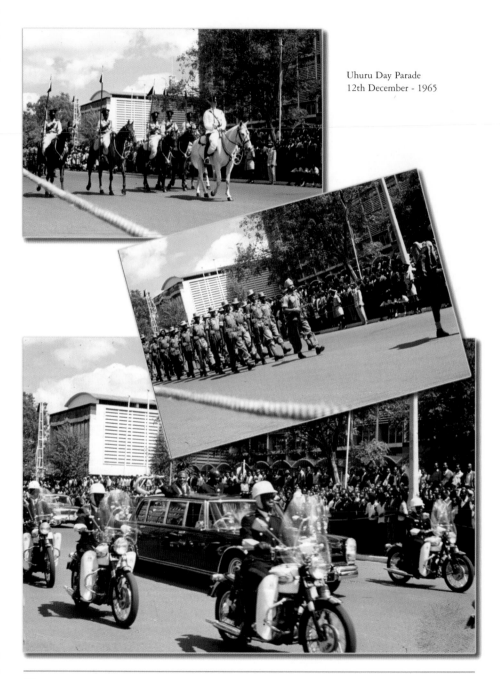

Uhuru Day Parade
12th December - 1965

Reparing "blown" culverts in Northern
Frontier District; Kenya - 1966

Building basic bridges

Water tanker in a land mine casualty

Somali work detail on way to quarry - Mandera

Quarry blasting

Mandera airstrip
under construction

First KAF Caribou cargo plane
lands at Mandera - 1966

Mandera and District
Commissioner's Office - 1966

KAF Beaver plane
- 1966

On patrol in NFD

A typical long distance
Kenyan bus journey

Ferry construction in Zambia

Zambezi River Patrol - 1970

My Lakka beach house
Sierra Leone

Later Murray town house
(with Erica)

Presidents Tolbert of Liberia and Stevens of Sierra Leone cross the
new Mano river road bridge joining two countries for the
first time in 1975. Built with SLOF gas. Did this road
bridge affect the later war from Libera?

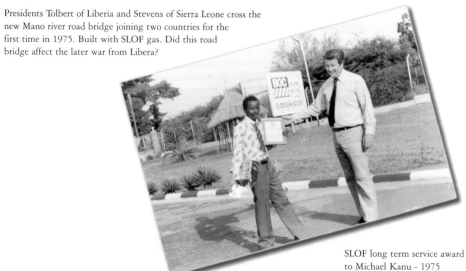

SLOF long term service award
to Michael Kanu - 1975

Chapter 6 - A civilian in Sierra Leone

Sierra Leone, named by Pedro daCintra, an early Portuguese explorer in 1462 after he saw the coast line resembled the silhouette of a sitting lion. There are and were no lions in Sierra Leone. Later settlers referred to it as the "Athens of West Africa". I have my doubts but never having visited Athens, am unable to comment!

I took over a mismanaged factory, riven by fear, in thrall to corrupt practices and a venal trades union. My predecessor was stretchered out so sedated as to be incapable of speech. Clearing out his desk of pornography, bundles of local currency tumbled out of the wall safe and every drawer. Soon returned paid overseas bank drafts began trickling through the post. Had my predecessor been diverting surplus funds through some private Middle Eastern bank, or was this some complicated Italian tax saving subterfuge? I never knew. The manufacturing part of the factory was run by two excitable Italians, technically competent engineers but with little English, less patience and perhaps even less social skills. Stock was obviously disappearing, the plant kept breaking down and staff strikes, walkouts and go slows were prevalent. I feigned ignorance of previous illicit practices, blindly determined to be the new broom. I had no idea how much 'sweeping' would be needed over the next years.

On arrival I stayed in the Paramount Hotel opposite State House which housed the Governor General Sir Banja Tejan-Sie, until he was deposed the following year. I was accompanied by my faithful, now aging, boxer-type dog Zimba who would sit on the hotel patio watching me. It was here that I first met Erica Powell - later to become a lifelong friend. I'd been previously advised to neither associate nor fraternise with this dangerous lady: "dowager of republicanism" as the more scurrilous free press referred to her. As with many deep friendships, it started unintentionally with a strong difference of opinion over the merits of keeping bitches over dogs. "Zimba" - although Swahili for a male lion, was in fact a bitch. We were both quite opinionated and begged to differ; I must have appeared insufferably arrogant and opinionated. It was an intriguing if slightly disturbing first introduction. There were others to avoid in the Paramount; once going up in the lift, a pretty local girl opened her coat to reveal herself to be quite naked underneath. *"What you see is what you get"* she intriguingly offered. After some weeks Erica moved out of the hotel to her allocated government house as she was employed by the President; this was sited close between the President's residence and a military barracks and I moved out to my new residence.

12 years of "living on the job" in the Army had had its disadvantages and for a number of other reasons I was unhappy to move into the residence of the previous Manager, a dockyard war-time pre-fabricated shack alongside the factory. Within a few weeks I rented a delightful small beach bungalow about ten miles south of Freetown. It was idyllic: a full length, covered veranda overlooking miles of empty untouched palm fringed, silver sands to the near hypnotic background of the gentle rolling breaking swish and sucking of an ebbing and flowing tide. It was part of an unfenced compound with three other houses owned by the retired Electricity Corporation Manager, Bruno-Gaston. This mini-estate had its our own generator but there was no telephone, so it promised real peace away from the stinking squalor and pervasive poverty of the raucous city. It was not so peaceful when my house was attacked during a noisy thunderstorm. A drug hyped, grease-smeared, near naked hired gang blew off the metal barred front door. Fortunately these were the days before the now ubiquitous AK47 and they only had machetes, but they would have considered themselves protected by a powerful magic juju. This was my warning. Twelve years of military service with its share of African senseless, grotesque horrors, torchings, maimings, decapitations and worse, had made me both resilient and self-reliant. Or was I just plain stubborn and didn't like to be intimidated? This stood me in good stead as that night I was repeatedly attacked until they must have become bored with me and locked me in a windowless store. They ransacked the rest of my house and left with their stolen goods in the company's Mercedes car. My neighbours had heard nothing; it was during a dramatic tropical storm. As day dawned I went to get some private medical attention. The British High Commission sent me a bottle of Champagne and the Police Commissioner an armed guard, for our own safety. After a few weeks I dispensed with the police guard's services when he shot at one of my visiting friends. The official gestures had been made. For days afterwards everyone I looked at seemed like members of this robber's gang.

Back at the factory, closer inspection revealed an obvious great hole in the company's finances. Sierra Leone was in the sterling area. Expatriate bosses who had illicitly removed funds were generally imprisoned during long investigations. Few prisoners without family, friends, food or finances survive long in African prisons. Freetown's Pademba Road prison was especially notorious and few left alive. This was not quite my idea of a civilian career so I returned to Italy, briefed my boss and resigned. This was no empty threat, I was serious. I was young and confident enough to be sure I could do something else. At their request the next day I drew up a "restart" plan which, after some discussion, was accepted. I got a new contract, an enhanced salary and benefits. I returned to Freetown with a document absolving me from all activities prior to my arrival. Michael, my accountant/auditor, who was to become my lifelong friend and supporter, redrew the accounts from a new day one. I relished this challenge against all odds and stayed for the next ten years. Eventually we had a safe, model factory with secure and generous employment contracts, free weekly laundered uniforms a resident tailor, a canteen, showers, medical welfare, supplementary education and pensions. I even became an accepted Trade Union trainer in health, safety and employment legislation. The "old" Trade Union had long since been discredited and their trouble-makers and thieves left with them, doubtless to better pickings elsewhere. Corruption was a way of life that permeated throughout society from the poda poda (mini-bus) boys who touted and collected fares: the fare was often doubled, half for the owner and half for the driver and tout boy. This could even apply to local flights where a valid boarding pass would not always assure your getting on the plane without an extra "inducement". In government pharmacies a long-awaited hard-won prescription from a doctor for medicines could often result in death. The pharmacist would charge for what should have been free, the patient would choose the cheapest medicine from the two or more prescribed. Even then when paying for four tablets they would only receive two. Living and working in a country where both corruption and patronage are the accepted way of life is never an easy tight-rope to walk. But I get ahead of the story.

Whilst I was at my out of town beach house there was another attempted coup. Erica, the lady I had disagreed with over dog care, was privately employed by the self-declared new President, Siaka Stevens, who had recently deposed the Governor General when unilaterally declaring Sierra Leone an independent Republic. This new Republic was distinctly unpopular with large sections of the educated populace, not least the elite Creoles. These were the descendants of freed slaves, often UK-educated professionals with anglicized slave hyphenated family names. They saw their dominant position threatened as the original "native" inhabitants began asserting themselves. To over simplify not everyone agreed with the new republic, hence the coup. Other dissidents and the ever present dispossessed always joined in; they had nothing to lose.

Erica's "official" job was to ghost write Stevens' autobiography, as she had previously done for President Kwame Nkrumah when she was his Private Secretary in Ghana. Newly emergent African Presidents seemed to favour a 'white' secretary, maybe it was a status thing. Her position in Sierra Leone was insecure and many, mistakenly, perceived her as a threat. Although the republic came sooner than expected, it had little to do with Erica. The perception the media often mischievously create by inference lets people believe what they want, truly a dark art. Stevens was a manipulative ex-Railway Trade Unionist who, after electing himself President, ran the country by patronage and had dark secrets on any potential challenger. He lost no time in consolidating his position by removing, often permanently, all opposition.

This attempted coup that brought Erica and me close was an attempt to remove the self-appointed President Stevens. It sounds blasé to say 'this coup', but coups were almost an annual event, generally brought on by the hot harmattan winds which preceded the rains when every-one became more short-tempered. President Stevens' colonial-style offices, ringed with outside balconies, had been surrounded by the military, although Stevens, with his ever prescient ability at longevity, had long since fled to neighbouring Guinea. Erica was sheltering behind her desk as the bullets peppered the building. Prior to the coup, Erica had attempted to visit the lavatory, which was behind her office and required her to walk along the outside front balcony, but the lavatory had been occupied. When the firing started some stray bullets pierced the lavatory cistern. Erica heard the water continuously running and it aggravated her desperation for a visit, but under the constant hail of bullets this was impossible. Needs must and Erica, ever the pragmatist, used an empty Nido powdered-milk can for relief. Telephones, with their haphazardly strung outside lines were never too reliable, yet incongruously, during civil disturbances, they seemed to work superbly. Erica's phone shrilled above the now sporadic gun fire; it was the British High Commissioner who promised to arrange a cease fire. The Army Commander Brigadier Bangura was Sandhurst trained and surely would not knowingly want to harm an English woman. The UNHCR High Commissioner then phoned to advise her to claim refugee status or political asylum. The firing stopped. The British High Commissioner phoned and told her she had five minutes to vacate the building. Clutching her Nido can, which she deposited at the bottom of the main outside staircase, Erica got in her reliable little Volkswagen, registered in Stevens' name. Pock marked but miraculously starting first time, she drove out of a deserted office through eerily empty streets of shuttered houses and shops to my beach house, and there she stayed for much of her time.

Over the years Erica became a good companion. An essentially private person she rarely spoke of her time in Ghana where she had initially gone as a pool typist in Governor General Arden Clark's office in pre-independence Gold Coast. Promoted to become the Governor General's Private Secretary she became friendly with Nkrumah until judged a security risk by the British Special Branch and deported back to the UK. Again this irrational colonial mentality and fear of expatriates becoming, "too close to the natives". On Nkrumah's release from jail and appointment as President, by prior agreement, Erica returned from the UK as his Private Secretary, to the obvious horror and consternation of the expatriate establishment set who had previously smirked and cut her dead. Nkrumah later died in exile in Guinea in 1972 when 52 and much later I would accompany Erica to his birth place in Nkroful, Ghana to visit Nkrumah's grave. We met Nkrumah's mother, whose soft hands smelt of sandalwood. Occasionally when we were alone and after a few whiskies, Erica would reminisce, generally happily, about her meeting President Chou-en-Lai of China, Tito, Louis Armstrong and Nixon and of her arrest in the Kremlin, where she claimed to be the first white woman to be arrested there since the anti-Tsarist revolutions of 1917.

My association with Erica brought a number of privileges, but at a price. We attended the State Opening of Parliament sitting in special seats together with a number of Paramount

Chiefs in their flowing heavy woven traditional costumes. Although ostensibly these seats were reserved there were never enough and a pompous UN official was remonstrating about being left standing. During the ceremony Erica picked up her hand bag and edged closer towards me on her right. Eventually the very elderly Paramount Chief to Erica's left, tottered out of his seat with his vacated place promptly being taken by the strutting UN official. Erica now leaning on me was struggling to maintain a suitably composed decorum, alternately crying and shaking with laughter, in order to befit the occasion - as the UN official, in his pristine lightweight white suit, sat in the spreading pool of urine from the departing incontinent Paramount Chief. After this ceremony waiting outside Parliament building through the crush of onlookers Erica was trying to get a photograph of the departing President and said to the security in what could be her rather imperious "jolly hockey sticks" voice *"Let me through, I need to get a shot at the President"* - deathly hush, perhaps not her best chosen phrase. Another morning Erica phoned me to join her at the Central Bank and I tagged on to the official, mainly government party. We went through many clanking safe doors into a vault and finally were passed around a fist sized lump that looked like a dirty misshapen block of ice. Unimpressed I was later told that this was the near thousand (968.9) carat "Star of Sierra Leone" diamond, worth a reputed US$ 6 million but sold to New York diamond broker Harry Winston's for an official US$2.5 million. No questions asked. I had not seen a diamond before and I remained unimpressed. No "diamond fever" gripped me as had happened to some expatriates. In Sierra Leone today's friend could be tomorrow's enemy and alliances could be short lived as loyalties were traded. Access to diamonds, quick fortunes, cheap lies and lives, treasons and traitors, plots and coups, cannibalism, drugs and black magic - all took their toll and made for strange bedfellows. Daily we were plagued with mischievous misunderstandings and potential dangers as we knew everyone had their price. Life was and continued to be cheap. Politicians nowhere have a secure tenure, even wily African despots, yet Stevens was a master and one of those few to die in office of old-age. I learnt the hard way to try and avoid too close a political affiliation, from anywhere. The only truly honest politician I have ever met I had worked with for over five years before I realized that he was an elected politician. Sadly he has just now retired, reputation intact; but more of him later.

I met a number of remarkable people with Erica, but perhaps the most surprising and memorable was the diminutive Hanna Reitsch. She was a German pilot who like so many of her fellow compatriots, had been a competition winning glider pilot prior to the war. She had been associated with the V2 pilotless bombers. Before they became fully pilot-less Hanna had test piloted the first V-bombers (V for vergeitungswaffe, vengeance weapon), during which many of her fellow test pilots had died. During the last days of the Third Reich she had incredibly landed a small plane in Unter den Linden Strasse in a bid to rescue Hitler from his Berlin bunker. This daring escapade is captured on a documentary film. When we all met in Frankfurt it was only a few years before her death in 1979, yet she was still a fiery and determined woman. Hanna still avowed she was no Nazi but a

German patriot – whatever; she was undeniably a striking, fearless and brave woman of great presence. Hanna helped found the fledging Ghanaian Air Force in the 1960s and had first met Erica there. I could understand how they were attracted to each other.

Sadly, Bangura, that Sandhurst trained Brigadier who had arranged the cease fire which saved Erica's life, was hanged as a traitor. A precursor of what was to become a pattern and a purge of many more Banguras. Refusing to empty the Central Bank reserve vaults for some Presidential whim or prestigious project, one early morning the Bank's Governor was found splattered and spread-eagled on the road far outside the bank compound high walls. He had failed to "fly" from the top of the multi storied Central bank building. Ask no questions and make no comments and no one seemed to raise an eyebrow, just another doomed Bangura. It was a Bangura youth whom we adopted into our lives, or perhaps, as so often happens in Africa, it was Brima who adopted us.

During my stay Sierra Leone changed from driving on the left side of the road to the right. The Minister of Transport infamously suggested that we should all start "practicing" before the changeover date; lorries three weeks before, minibuses and taxis two weeks before and private cars a week before. In any event driving ordinarily in Sierra Leone was a lawless nightmare, whatever side of the road. Our company had two drivers ostensibly to cover shifts but more often than not to cover arbitrary arrests or detentions. Vehicle lights were kicked in so as to impound the vehicle as unsafe, occasionally an angry crowd would roll our car over, when once they thought we had stocks of free T-shirts inside, not fun as a passenger. Safety belts recommended! There was just one set of traffic lights in Freetown controlling traffic over a long single lane bridge. Once the police had worked out how to set both lights permanently at red it proved to be a real money earner for them. We imported one of the first new Range Rovers as our Italian boss liked to go hunting up-country. To assess it for import duty, whether as a car or a utility vehicle, it was borrowed by a politician. After a long time it came back sporting bullet holes, which did little for its new air conditioning. The heavy air conditioning unit was mounted on the roof, making the whole vehicle inherently unstable. A palm wine tapper once drunkenly fell out of a tree and staggered into our car, to die in hospital a few days later. Our car was impounded and the driver arrested for manslaughter, despite the unfortunate palm wine tapper actually dying of gangrene from his untreated wounds. Our allowances scale included a special per diem rate for overnight in a police cell. Percy Ayomi Johnson, our loyal "Mr Fix it", was a retired ex United Africa Company manager who also looked after things in my absence on leave. He had the lovely maxim that any problem was ignored until it went away, or became so big someone else had to sort it out. Not exactly my style, but I learnt to live with it. God bless you dear Percy, you taught me much about survival.

Following the attack on my house I was advised and allowed to get a hand gun. I had mixed feelings about this and was developing a healthy hatred for all weapons. I decided to buy one, not necessarily to use it, but in my mistaken perception of its deterrent value.

Surprisingly I did this with the minimum of fuss in what appeared to be an ordinary shop in Piccadilly, London. To test fire the merchandise there was even a shooting range in the cellars. I was assured that my gun would be at the airport for my flight back. In the event "the package" missed my flight and I re-arranged for it to be with me on a subsequent flight. For this second flight I identified the package and the airline flight crew took charge of it. I was used to this procedure having previously travelled extensively by air with a ceremonial military sword, classed as an offensive weapon, which the flight crew took charge of. I'm not sure if any plane has yet had an attempted hi-jacking with a ceremonial sword, although I know that an Ethiopian once attempted to hi-jack a plane with the plastic cutlery provided in flight. I flew from London and changed to a UTA flight in Paris. In the Paris transit lounge the British airline crew gave me the package and ammunition with instructions to hand it to the UTA flight crew. There was some delay in my boarding the UTA flight due to an over booking. Finally, at the last moment, I was called and on approaching the metal detector declared my package. *"I have a pistol"* I said, innocently enough. Airport chaos ensued and I count myself lucky that I was finally allowed to get on the by now much delayed flight. The pistol was openly handed over to me by the flight crew as I left the aircraft in Freetown. I never used this pistol, apart from occasionally shooting at beer cans. In fact if owning the gun was meant to give me confidence it did not, and I felt distinctly uncomfortable owning it. I thought I had given up guns when I left the army and was then and am now of the view that guns can only escalate violence; never preventing it. On leaving Sierra Leone I gave the gun to Percy. Whether he or his sons ever used it for real in the subsequent eight year civil war, I do not want to know.

I flew (and fly) a lot and can never quite anticipate or gauge customs searches. Experience now suggests to me to always expect the unexpected and that you will be searched. Once arriving from Sierra Leone I had rather a large sum of UK sterling with me hidden inside a hollowed out large book. In Sierra Leone I did not take the book on to the plane myself, too risky, but it was brought to me by my friend Mo an albino airport health official who was the last official on the plane; he had to spray the plane with anti-malarial spray just before it took off. The procedure we agreed was that he handed me the book which "I'd forgotten in the VIP lounge", I had to trust him totally, but he'd never let me down. Did Mo ever know what was in the book? Maybe, maybe not; there are some things you just never talk about. If he was caught there was more than enough money for him to buy his way out of any problem. If I was implicated, well it could have been very different. I flew into Heathrow via Amsterdam one cold early morning and for no given reason was singled out and taken to a bleak stale smelling unheated partitioned room. I had only hand luggage as had recently returned from the UK; officially I was returning to sign an agency distribution agreement with a UK company. My brief case was thoroughly searched and I was then stripped to my underpants, even the seams of my pants were felt by one officer with another in attendance feigning disinterest. My bare feet were freezing on the cold linoleum floor. Of course the book was found and the money counted - but returned to me intact. Were these officials smirking or actually smiling? Apparently It was no offence to bring the money in, but would certainly have been an offence to take it out of Sierra Leone. Customs kept (or is seized the right word?) the book "for our museum" they said. I had no problem with that; I certainly did not anticipate to be using this method again. A bank counter was open in the airport and I immediately paid all the money in - to the credit of my Italian bosses account; it was to help pay an Italian Red Brigade kidnap ransom for my bosses daughter, but more of that later.

Phone conversations, local or international were routinely recorded by the faceless "security"; we learnt to talk obliquely, in code or using euphemisms. Returning on UK leave, friends chastised me for unknowingly continuing this practice. *"We'll meet at the same place as yesterday"* I would say. During one long call to my boss in Italy, the "listener" interrupted, requesting a pause whilst he put in a new tape. Suddenly we had little more to say to each other.

Joyce Welch, another English woman who had also worked in Ghana, was the Secretary to Sierra Leone's Prime Minister. She often joined our small circle, drinking local gin with *"only a dash of tonic"*. Joyce went back to the UK with cancer but was denied free government treatment. Essentially single - her husband had not returned from the war, *"not died"*, she insisted, and we knew of no other living relatives. She returned to Freetown she said, unsentimentally, to die among friends. She lived in two small adjoining rented rooms on the first floor of a traditional clap board Creole house. She died one Saturday evening, alone. On her lap she had been reading a book I had lent her - "Hold my hand, I'm dying" set during the Rhodesian civil war. No one was holding her hand. Although not yet ready, there is still far too much still to do, I am not afraid of dying but I would prefer not to die alone, or take too long over it. We called the undertakers who came and one of them slung her skeletal body over his shoulders. With some difficulty we persuaded the undertaker's assistant to carry her body down the outside staircase with perhaps just a little more dignity. Awaiting authority from her executors in the UK to carry out her burial, she stayed for a long time in a thankfully refrigerated funeral home which had its own generator. This was an experience in itself with its ever changing "residents" and accompanying taped "heavenly music". Every day when I visited, the coffin had been re-opened and she had been re-dressed in newer clothes with fresh bunches of flowers stuck in her folded and newly gloved hands. Death in Sierra Leone amongst the Creole community has a whole procedure of its own. Finally through the British High Commission, we learnt that her UK executors had authorised Joyce's burial. We were to pay for the funeral "from her personal effects". There were none. Erica and I had basically furnished her rooms and Immediately after her death her "boy" had removed whatever was portable, clothes, radio, lamps, etc., that he could carry. The perception that all expatriates get rich in Africa is not correct. For her to have died alone I still find guiltily disturbing. Later the Prime Minister Sorie Ibrahim Kamara touchingly paid for Joyce's engraved grave head-stone, one of the few items allowed to be imported duty free. Her grave is now surrounded by thousands of dead soldiers' graves from their recent civil wars. Decades later I had to "pay" some cartons of cigarettes as entry fee to be allowed to visit her grave in this cemetery.

Death, particularly in Sierra Leone, can often seem bizarre with a strange mixture of ritual both casual and formal, Christian and pagan. One day a factory labourer came into my office formally requesting a loan and the day off for his new stillborn baby. This was usually automatically given. He had his baby wrapped in a string-tied paper parcel he was carrying in a plastic bag. Freetown is a crowded city where all live cheek by jowl, yet there are huge expanses of land dedicated to cemeteries. Generally dead people are buried immediately, or at latest the next day, but on their way to the cemetery pall bearers have been known to turn round as directed by deceased spirits of those they were carrying. Grave site visits are regularly undertaken when small bottles of gin or other spirits are left for the deceased to assuage the thirst of the dead and appease their spirits. Great ceremonies are held at seven days (the soul leaving the body) and at forty days (when it arrives in heaven). Food is buried for the deceased at annual ceremonies for many years afterwards. You just have to join in, wear the right dark formal suits and ties, say the right things and, for me, be an uncomfortable hypocrite. But it is not only in Africa that death is treated strangely. I had an Anglo-Indian cousin who, convinced he would not be revered with due respect after his death, had not only already booked his burial plot in a prestigious London cemetery but also had the gravestone erected and engraved with all his details "Deeply beloved husband and father, much missed etc..." everything in fact except his date of death. Towards his end he used to sit for days by this gravestone and gain some sort of peace and solace. Apparently a young visiting Australian couple were searching the cemetery looking for an old relative's grave and came across this incomplete gravestone with cousin dozing on a bench alongside. Commenting on this unusual, unfinished grave stone that had no date of death, our cousin, now a gaunt looking pale-yellow, woke up and said *"This is my grave"*. Fast exit two deeply disturbed Australians.

For Erica ghosting the autobiography of this self-professed largely unread Stevens, who once openly decried education and confessed that he was "not a book person", could not have been easy. His throw away "not a book person" comment resulted in a full blown riot. The entire centuries-old, irreplaceable book collection from the long-established Fourah Bay College University library was dragged out and ceremoniously burnt by the illiterate paramilitaries. Educated and professional people were suspect and systematically harassed, sometimes terminally, if not given the kinder opportunity and rare option of being able to leave the country. What an incredibly sad waste of resources. It was no wonder that those I sent overseas for higher education, so as to ultimately take over from me, failed to return. Putting a draft copy of a chapter of the autobiography manuscript on Stevens' desk, Erica was appalled to see an execution order, already signed, for 15 or more of these dissident overseas educated "traitors". Following their mock trial they were all being held in the notorious Pademba Road jail. All were academics or professionals, and generally known personally to Erica. A clandestine discreet meeting was arranged with the British High Commissioner in as neutral location as we could manage. A high level personal petition for clemency from five world leaders including Kurt Waldheim the UN Secretary General, was made to the President's office. That it was ignored or failed is another stain of international indifference. After the spectacle of a public midnight hanging, we later met the appointed certifying doctor, a Sri Lankan medical orderly locally made up to "Doctor". In an alcoholic stupor and, perhaps plagued by his conscience, he confessed to Erica and me that four of those executions he had certified had been tortured to death prior to their "execution". This was almost as ghoulish as the English disinterring Oliver Cromwell years after his death to "draw and quarter" his decomposed body before publicly displaying it for his part in King Charles I execution. Unsurprising as this revelation was, it compounded our horror. Erica, torn by her divided loyalties and appalled at the senseless brutality of it all, ultimately left Sierra Leone in 1977. Her plagiarised manuscript was published in 1984 as "What life has taught me", with no attribution to Erica. Critics panned it as "bland and unrevealing". But then Stevens never revealed much.

Sierra Leone was a country of continual intrigue; Saturday was a free day in every sense of the word. Few adult men slept at home on a Saturday night. This was also the favourite night for a coup as people were out and if not drunk often intoxicated; coups were usually prefaced with a power cut. Coups were externally instigated. Those local helpers were generally well rewarded with overseas shopping trips, family educational scholarships, long-term visas and often serious money. My Trade Unionist links with those who threw the power switches gave me coded phoned warnings. I was driving one early evening to collect Erica for safety as Erica's house was too near the President's residence and overlooked by a military barracks, so not the best place to be. Shooting during coups was wild rather than personal or vindictive, but no less lethal. I was running late and whatever route I took I had to pass either the military barracks or the President's compound, neither good. I chose the shorter route to pass the Presidential compound. I had probably drunk too much. Foolishly I was alone and, even more foolishly; I was driving an open-topped Mercedes. The constant threat and strain of always "being ready" could make you careless and alcohol could cloud judgement. The power had already been cut and the entire city had been thrown into darkness with mass panic as streets emptied and shutters came down. As I approached the Presidential compound I noted that his generator had not tripped in, which was not a good sign. At the military road block my car horn jammed on, which was the cue for near panic by the illiterate, trigger-happy, nervous Presidential guards. I was desperately aware that I must neither appear too clever nor too smart. My pistol was under my car seat, but I was sure I would neither show nor use it, even if the opportunity arose. I got out of the car slowly showing my empty hands, opened the bonnet carefully, pulled off the horn wires and drove away very slowly. That was another close call but how long could my luck last?

Saturday was a serious drinking day, starting at or about noon. When the Elder Dempster passenger and cargo boats still called, it was their flagship the SS Aureol in the 1970s, we would go on board and drink draught beer, ostensibly to see friends off. Afterwards I went with my friend Percy to a small side street private Creole house where we drank bottled beer and ate skewered chicken kebabs rolled in eye watering chilli sauce. It was years later before I realised that this house belonged to Percy's official mistress. Mistresses were accepted in a very mature and civilized way and she had a lovely and fully recognised son Arthur whom Percy maintained. Saturday afternoons, if there was no football to entertain, could develop into a rioting day. A losing gang would rush through the front public shop and into our private drinking room, strip off all their clothes, and do a quick change to re-emerge on the street in the winning or stronger side's "strip". APC was red, SLPP was green, and their quick change would credit any professional artiste or magician. It could be mildly entertaining if it did not so often result in tragedy.

But if Saturday was a drinking day, Sunday in Freetown was a church day. Out came all the black outfits and, for ladies, big hats and face nets. Was this to sing away the sins of yesterday? But Creole churches with their beautiful angelic choirs were hardly places of love, more of fear. Flapping black-garbed priests harangued us with hell-fire and eternal damnation beneath banners proclaiming "The Wages of Sin are death" and such like. I found this a little inappropriate when morning services were often immediately followed by christenings.

As an active, enquiring, sixty year-old, my mother visited Sierra Leone twice. One day in order to visit my own company driver's mother; we took an old motor boat across the wide Freetown bay and up a little tidal creek to her village at Menika. This otherwise isolated inaccessible village had never seen such an elderly, very white haired, pale woman. We had arrived at low tide and it was quite an event as mother was carried shoulder high through the oozing mud. Their kind acceptance and hospitality was deeply touching. The only village chair was solicitously produced. A squawking chicken was caught and a few hours later a tasty ground nut (peanut mixed with palm oil) stew was served with fluffy rice. It was midday and hot, even in this shady village; mother dozed off. She was surrounded at a respectful distance by a semi-circle of gazing eyes; all were very quiet. A puzzling question from the older men revealed that they thought Queen Elizabeth II of England had come to visit. A few years earlier the Queen of England had in fact visited the nearby Delco Iron Ore mine at Lunsar. Incongruously wearing a long formal dress and a tiara she had addressed the crowd of thousands of workers from a platform erected on top of a waste slag heap. Was she not a little over dressed I asked an High Commission employee, *"No"* he explained, *"she must look like her posters and wear a crown, otherwise they won't believe that she's the Queen"*. When the Menika villagers were finally dissuaded that my mother was neither the Queen nor any great personage, they seemed both confused and disappointed *"But why has the Queen forsaken us?"* they asked. They had heard that the country now had a new President, but were obviously still ardent Royalists. Mother managed her part well, although did admit to finding the screeching monkeys a little disconcerting when she had to squat for a call of nature behind a bush. *"They are laughing at me"* Mum remarked; probably they had never seen a white backside before.

On the cul-de-sac approaching my beach house we had to pass an isolation hospital. During a particularly virulent cholera epidemic a derelict roofless shack was being used as a holding area where shrouded bodies were stacked on top of each other awaiting some sort of irregular collection or disposal. How much mother saw, or understood, she never said. Whilst I was at work, mother took long beach walks. Apart from a few isolated fishermen, the five miles of beach was usually deserted. The shoreline villages not so, and she was always faithfully shadowed by our gardener Amadou Bah. This was active cannibal country and strangers were often favoured prey. A few years earlier an entire fishing village had all been imprisoned on suspicion of cannibalism. Later they all died in Pademba Road prison before their case even came to court. If you lock men up who are used to being free they can lose the will to live.

When mother visited again I had moved to larger house in Murray Town, a part of Freetown city. It stood on a prominent cliff overlooking the wide Sierra Leone River, said to be the third largest natural harbour in the world. I loved to watch the huge liners, freighters and tankers round Cape Sierra and pass the evocatively named Pirate Bay and Man o'War Bay. In a way it helped me feel in touch with the rest of the real world outside. My neighbours were, on one side, an affable Russian Ambassador and his wife, both true anglophiles who had spent many years in, and missed, their Kensington London Embassy and, on the other, the Yellow Submarine Night Club and Casino. My Italian boss, whom we referred to as Dottore Franco, was visiting at the same time as mother who, trying to start some small talk, asked if this was his first visit to Sierra Leone. With his beautiful quiet old world gentle courtesy he pointed to Cape Sierra and replied: *"No, not actually Madam."* As a submarine commander he had stood off that point, trying unsuccessfully to breach the British naval defences in 1941: *"I thought Sierra Leone looked beautiful then, and I still do"* he continued.

We were installing a piped oxygen supply to the main local hospital's new intensive care ward. As I visited this project snarling feral dogs slunk past me with prized amputated human limbs and equally feral street kids scavenged through dumps of broken phials, needles and stained bandages. Until we put metal doors on our oxygen gas-store out-building it was used as a lavatory and general dumping ground, in every sense of the word. This was to be another typical government project for which we could never expect to be paid and I came to look on these more as social projects. The tortuous process of handing out wearying "facilitation fees" through the many layers of poorly or unpaid civil servants' outstretched hands seemed no longer worth the time and effort on these smaller contracts. We already supplied oxygen to most government hospitals with little hope of receiving payment. All government offices were vastly over staffed, generally through nepotism. Desks would not be filled so much with papers but people lounging all over and even under them. Percy normally handled all government office business. When alone, for me to get a required authority or recommendation letter written by any Minister, I ended up bringing the paper, new typewriter ribbon, rubber stamp pad and envelope, plus of course the requisite stuffed brown envelope to make it "worth the typists time". Our product, being locally manufactured, was a government price-controlled commodity so to get a price rise it had to be authorised by the Minister of Trade and Industry. Percy reported that the Minister required a generator for his local village health centre to "help" process our application. Of course there was no village health centre, but he had his family house there and needs must. The generator was supplied just as the Minister was appointed to another ministry so we got no price rise. A little later the Minister died a long, lingering death, either by poisoned food or, a Sierra Leone favourite, eating ground glass. Percy said it was divine retribution. I began to wonder and almost admire the longevity of the President even more. Subject to constant attempted coups and poisonings he finally died of old age in 1988; a wily man.

A US commercial visitor from Dupont, for whose chemicals and Freon gases we were agents, was staying in my house. In fact he over stayed as, due to a coup in Nigeria his next destination, his departure was delayed for some weeks until the country settled down to normality and the airports reopened. Later, visiting their Head Office in Philadelphia, Pennsylvania, I read his report on Sierra Leone where I was referred to as a neo-colonialist despot. Thank you: it gave me much food for introspective thought. Subsequently, visitors who were not family or close friends stayed in hotels, of which there were now many - both hotels and visitors. True, I employed a large house staff, but they were well paid, had their own compound with their own rooms, a kitchen, a shower and an ample continual supply of their staple food, rice. That I was constantly short changed I accepted, within limits. Visitors to their compound were unrestricted, alcohol or too much noise was not encouraged, but I was realistic and whilst I was there I had no staff turnover.

While it was still relatively safe to travel I went on "export" missions to neighbouring countries, sometimes government sponsored, sometimes privately. Before road blocks became too intrusive, too many or too dangerous, we drove. Afterwards I took local flights. Interflug was an East German airline that flew locally. Their huge, noisy, propeller driven aircraft flew at palm tree top level. Inside there were slatted wooden seats rather like the old Leeds trams. In flight they gave you a huge bottle of East German beer, a Dresden lace handkerchief and a packet of East German cigarettes. In-flight smoking was allowed but fortunately flights were only a few minutes. In Liberia MPs still wore top hats and tails to their offices and it seemed they had imported everything distasteful and worse from the United States; they were even still using US dollar currency. That they were so very different from neighbouring Sierra Leone, yet still from that "freed slave" background, was intriguing if not a little unnerving. Guinea to the north had a command economy and even for a modest meal we had to carry large bundles of devalued currency in huge holdalls or suit-cases. We were constantly shadowed by their easy to spot security; it was often more practical to identify your tail and take him with you. We had been advised that all hotel staff were retained informers.

As with most British colonies a railway had been built and was still operating moderately efficiently in Sierra Leone. It had a very narrow gauge so that, it was said, the French, who had colonised Guinea to the north and east, could not link up to their wider gauge railway and come storming into the capital. But perhaps its narrow gauge made it easier to negotiate bends and gradients. In 1970 this was still working well, but as a precondition for a German aid new road construction programme there was the stipulation that the railway must be shut down. The illogicality of this, as the road programme would not be where the railway was and that the population and goods access to markets would be lost, defies comment. Erica and I travelled on the last train in 1971, pulled by a locomotive recently manufactured in Hunslet, Leeds. It was an emotional trip; every station manned by smart, starched khaki-clad staff and hundreds of cheering bystanders. Local national flights were much quicker if not always safer and operated by Sierra Leone Airways, until the airline was sold to an investor who promptly flew all their Otter prop-driven planes out of the country - never to return. The pilots were usually aging, intemperate expatriates and I doubt they were ever breath tested. Once, taking off we were half way down Hastings dirt airstrip when we skidded to a sideways halt. The scarlet faced, angry pilot got out and berated a herd boy for letting his goat herd cross the runway. He then climbed back in and continued to take off from half way down the strip, the under-carriage narrowly clipping the strip-end palm trees. Not reassuring. Perhaps road travel was the safer option after all!

As elected President of the local Rotary Club for a year I managed to instigate a few worthwhile social projects, certainly there was enough demand. I had strongly encouraged and supported overseas post graduate scholarships for local bright youngsters and for this the Club awarded me the Rotary Paul Harris Fellowship medal. Sadly few of the scholarship recipients returned to use their new-found knowledge to benefit their country. Privately I was locally supporting the Milton Margai School for the Deaf where the Rotary Club had built and equipped a kitchen to allow the students to have on-site cooked midday meals. At the British Council I enjoyed amateur dramatics; this was real escapism, although I was never sure what our local audit team thought of my performance as the embezzling convicted forger in "My Three Angels". Was it wise to have given them free tickets during our annual audit?

How I came to sponsor a Guinean traditional bare-breasted dance troupe I can't honestly recall. Certainly most of my house staff were Guinean as they were generally more honest. I used to arrange dock side dance performances for visiting tour ships and, later, local TV appearances. Their traditional music was beautiful and quite haunting. I made sure they earned enough to feed themselves, although they lived simply in a nearby forest; they must have been refugees.

Essentially I began to feel increasingly uncomfortable and tainted by this rather decadent distinctly privileged life of richness, insecure as it was. Regardless of all the trappings that came with big cars, motor cruisers, and living in large, over-staffed, air-conditioned houses with swimming pools, it brought little lasting or deep joy. Outside our secure high-walled compounds we were surrounded, as in Kenya and Zambia, by the stench and squalor of unremitting and abject poverty. Only in Sierra Leone the intense humidity made it all seem more pervasive and difficult to bear. This was a country of near anarchy and no shame, unremitting begging, blatant evil, intrigues, plotting and public executions.

Yet incredibly through all this poverty and madness; there shone that unquenchable thirst of all Africans for knowledge. For Sierra Leoneans this often meant leaving to study overseas. Knowledge was power, wealth and a better future, but for the masses access to it was never easy and it never came free. Decades later, throughout Africa, this has not changed. Many Sierra Leoneans often start by begging to be taken to the UK and, after endless parrying, end up by asking for a few notes. *"No money oh"*, was greeted derisively with *"White men get big pockets"*.

I was never sick so it was unusual for me when I once had a fever and temperature of 104°F. Our usual Lebanese doctor was out of the country, but whoever I saw gave me an injection and told me to go home and to bed. I must have become quite delirious and I vaguely remember Erica and my lovely neighbour Muriel Stanley sitting either side of my bed to watch over me. I think they consumed a bottle of Chivas Regal that night as they were hilariously drunk and noisy as they endlessly related tasteless hospital jokes. I seem to have lost the power or will to speak, but I distinctly remember thinking how bad they would feel in the morning as I most certainly would be lying dead. With dawn my fever had broken and they both were suffering from the crippling hangovers. I felt it was poetic justice and they received little sympathy from me.

Despite Sierra Leone being referred to as the Athens of West Africa, most expatriates from the 18th and 19th centuries rarely lived beyond their thirties and there was never a settler community as in East or South Africa. Malaria was rife and there were those that thought the mosquito had saved the country from expatriate settlers and domination. Newly independent Sierra Leone even cast a medal, the Mosquito Medal or MM, to commemorate this liberating insect.

Yet Sierra Leone was the land of proclaimed freedom for liberated slaves. The land for Freetown had been bought from a local chief called King Tom and named just for this, but it hid a murky history. At night wailing ghosts and sounds of dragging slave chains were commonplace where I lived by the sea, but now in a city house surrounded by cemeteries. One unusually stormier night than most, my house roof was blown off. I had returned late from the end of some amateur theatrical performance in the British Council; probably I was not in the best condition. I lay on my bed staring at the stars as it rained on me.

The monkeys I kept had escaped and were tapping on the bedroom window. Was this nightmare or reality? My two Guinean Fula night security guards had been unable to start the backup generator and, not unusually, had flat batteries in their torches, invariably used up in their radios. I stumbled down to open the front door to give my torch to the guards when some wild creature leapt in, scratching my sweating naked back. I could feel warm blood trickling down to my wrap. The guards, flailing their night sticks, came in to the dark front room and every stick of furniture, glass topped tables and a bar was quite destroyed. The "witch" had been destroyed, although in the cold light of morning it turned out to be little more than a rather large wild cat. In a land where snakes, when shot, turn into people, it was not unusual for witches, when bagged, to turn into cats. Finally persuaded, I paid a small amount of money for our supposedly cursed compound to be locally "cleansed". I went away for a few days whilst this took place. Believe what you will, sometimes it is better not to look for too logical a "Western" explanation. I remembered my Kenyan Army storekeeper who had convinced himself that he and his family were cursed, and they had all died. Stranger unexplained things were to happen later in both Indonesia and Ethiopia, often to highly intelligent western-educated local people. I began to appreciate and have a grudging respect for white, black and grey magic. I will risk criticism, but to me there are similarities between magic and religion. If you have faith and believe, it can work, for or against you. The Minister of Information was convicted of cannibalism and hanged. Losing his sexual prowess, vital to the machismo of all African men, he had obtained those necessary parts of a young boy to eat. In court the bewildered boy's parents could not understand; they were so proud that their son had been "chosen" by this big man, and they had even been paid ten Leones (about £5). Another politician was found to have a freezer full of young girls, as reserves he explained. Following this court case and conviction, freezers were ordered not by cubic foot size but by a child's age. Perhaps this decidedly sick humour helped us to cope with such atrocities. Other macabre horrors witnessed about child witches and soldiers are still too uncomfortable to write about. During their eight year destructive civil war these strange unfathomable and, to the outside world, unjustifiable inhuman practices remain just that - unjustifiable and barely credible.

The country's electricity supply was mainly diesel generated (it only had a small hydro electric plant) and was at best erratic. Payment for the fuel to power the generators was often delayed or misappropriated and supplies were cut off. Our factory had long since purchased a powerful Rolls Royce generator, well maintained and still going strong after over 40 years. The use of lifts, often poorly maintained, was distinctly risky and ill advised. One expatriate mining engineer, stuck in a lift during a power cut, managed to prise the doors open between floors and was getting out backwards. The power supply suddenly came back on, the lift doors clammed shut and he was decapitated. His severed head went up to the sixth floor where his wife was patiently waiting.

Our factory produced a waste from acetylene production. It was used for marking our football pitch and was in fact whitewash. It was not only wasted but polluting as it seeped into the estuary. Digging a sediment pit allowed it to settle. We allowed Sanussi a market trader to freely collect it for his marketing and a small business was born. As an excise factory we had a resident excise officer who assessed and levied an ad valorem tax on all we produced. Protracted bureaucratic deliberations decreed that we should record all whitewash production for an excise levy. Later they appreciated that an 8% excise duty on a zero valued "sale" was zero, but as a face saving exercise we were still obliged to keep records of all transactions. This is not an attitude peculiar to either Sierra Leone or Africa. Some find it difficult to accept that things may be done for an altruistic non-selfish reason. I am often asked, now retired, why I run a charity when I could relax, read, play golf or whatever. Any explanation is usually greeted by a silent disbelief. Perhaps it is assumed I am making a private fortune, as thought of many expatriates who work overseas.

As a result of my work with and support for the Milton Margai School for the Deaf, we had employed Huddy, one of their graduated students as a store-keeper. All storekeepers, whether military, civilian or humanitarian, jealousy guard their stores and always seem averse to issuing anything, and this guy was no exception. Adept at using his disability to his advantage, Huddy was an expert intelligent lip-reader quick to grasp anything. Yet he could become very deaf when a request was made to issue an item he didn't wish to. An exceptionally talented football player, once he had possession of the ball he'd go quite deaf and forget the team until he'd scored.

I have never assumed any African employment contract I had was permanent. I always felt that my time was best served to train and fit local indigenous people to replace me as soon as practicable. I sent potential senior manager replacements for overseas training, but after graduation they invariably failed to return, perhaps unsurprisingly. Training another, Philip Lamin, at the local university was similarly fraught following local student unrest. Most African leaders and regimes have fallen following impressionable students' riots, so government reaction is often brutal and mercilessly savage. Although Lamin is now teaching in Canada, remarkably the factory survived virtually intact following Sierra Leone's Liberian inspired barbarous drug and diamond-fuelled eight year civil war in which so much good was so senselessly destroyed. Over 30 years later the factory is still managed by Reginald Wilhelm, one of those first grammar school youngsters I had interviewed, employed and trained. I firmly believe that this is a living testament of hope and a better future through education and the indomitable spirit of Africans. Sadly now the factory's adjoining football field is an overcrowded tented refugee camp full of civil war amputees, rape victims and abandoned orphaned youngsters.

Flying further afield around West Africa beyond the adjoining states of Guinea and Liberia was never straight forward. Each country had their own national carrier and there was little coordination and few inter country flights connected, it was rather like travelling by bus and train in the UK today. This generally required an overnight stop in every country which meant the excitement of customs probes, currency declarations and the airport taxi touts. Notably during a dinner in an Accra hotel the menu card was taken away, prices adjusted upwards and returned. I had to pay the new price, inflation in action. More embarrassing was playing roulette in the hotel casino as however wildly I gambled and tried to get rid of an ever increasing pile of Cedis, I kept winning. In the morning I hired a taxi to view the "tourist" sites and go on a spending spree, but there was little to buy and despite my best efforts I still had more currency than on my declaration form when I checked in at the airport to leave. This was an unaccustomed dilemma: to hand over my surplus Cedis and be accused of an attempted bribery or to try to give it away without causing a riot. Whilst I really do not approve of gambling, I do always seem to have been lucky at chance. My best raffle ticket win was a trip to the US on the liner QE2 with a return on the newly launched Concord. Mid Atlantic the QE2 stopped for two days and some UK military commandos arrived by helicopter. We were told later that there had been a bomb alert. No bomb was found but I used the time profitably to win the backgammon championships and get the prize of a carton of bourbon. Due to our delay we were unable to return on the scheduled British Airways Concord so returned by Air France, which I was told served better food. Sadly no French cheese was served as the two hour flight time pre-empted time for a full dinner. A comment on leaving the plane in Paris from a US passenger was his joy at being able to smoke a Cuban cigar for the first time in over ten years; it's always important to get things in perspective.

Cousin Geoff asked my views on working in Africa and I had enthused. He was an industrial chemical engineer born in South America with overseas experience working in Europe and North America. He worked as an industrial chemist in many paint factories in three countries, training Africans until they took over. Much of what is manufactured in Africa is made from expensively imported commodities. Until he retired many decades later and long before re-cycling became fashionable, with a local partner Geoff successfully started a small factory, producing putty out of waste sludge oil and old vehicle tyres. This type of small business venture utilising what is locally available is commendable. Developing countries have always been far better at innovation and re-cycling than I fear we in the west will ever be. Geoff always appreciated the African's ability, and nurtured and developed it. He could be single-minded and stubborn but I greatly admired Geoff's practical respect of and for Africans. For a time he joined the board of the charity African Children's Educational Trust (A-CET), until sadly a heart attack precluded him taking a full part in our activities.

The 11 year old young lad, who adopted us, Brima, at his request, followed us back to the UK to complete his education. As the Immigration authorities and subsequent Tribunal refused our application, he was never formally adopted. Erica and I, as unmarried, were deemed to be living in sin and so were morally unsuitable to be adoptive parents; this was still the early seventies. We were later advised that a white couple adopting a black child was also thought unacceptable. By the time our appeal was finally accepted, Brima was, at 18, beyond adoption age. By then he was serving overseas in the British Army. Despite or because of our experiences I am very hesitant and have grave reservations about all overseas adoptions. Adopting mature children from overseas has even more problems than adopting babies. On arrival in any foreign country an adopted child must bear an incredible loneliness and throughout their life a continuing cultural identity crisis. After some years Brima was invalided out of the forces on a disability pension following a botched naval hospital operation in which he effectively lost the full use of his right hand. Fortunately he is at least left handed. Now a long established Essex business proprietor, I'm very proud of his positive contribution to the UK and his personal achievements. He steadfastly refuses to take any benefits he is entitled to; not all immigrants are worthless scroungers. In many ways I often feel that Brima is far more British than I am. I feel assured that his quality of life is certainly better than had he stayed in Freetown, better and very different.

My promised transfer and promotion from Sierra Leone to a proposed new factory in Kaduna, Northern Nigeria was continually postponed. My Italian boss's daughter had been kidnapped by the Red Brigade, and all his company's funds for future investment were on hold. Required to pay an exorbitant ransom for her eventual safe release, the new factory remained an impossible dream.

Twice I've been counted in an African population census and I can but wonder at the wisdom and accuracy of taking the count on the basis of "where were you on Saturday night"? In Africa this is a night where sleeping around for most men is more than usual. This must have recorded many double entries, in every sense!

The factory was running well, there was a Sierra Leonean Engineer recruited from the UK and all local management and staff were reasonably competent and within the Sierra Leonean context as honest as conditions allowed. I felt there was little challenge left for me and with Erica already in the UK it was time to move on. Unfulfilled, unfocussed and only dimly determined to do "something different to help change African people's lives for the better", I left. There was little here for me any more and it was to be some time before I returned to help reintegrate and educate demobilized child soldiers, both boys and girls.

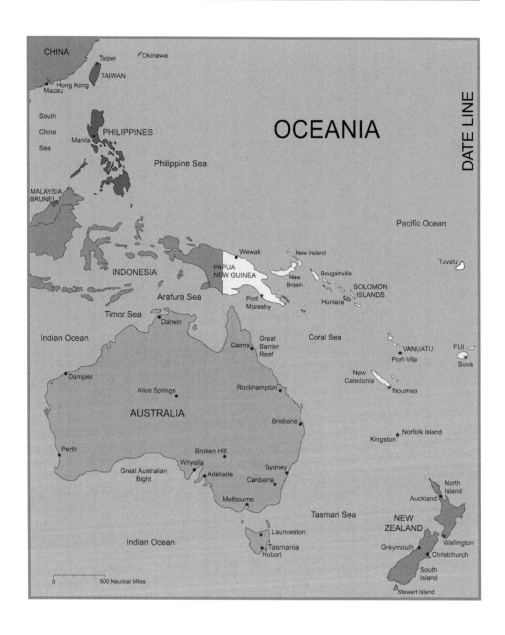

Chapter 7 - UK - with a spell in the South Pacific

Back in the UK for a time, Erica and I ran a small, award winning, convenience store, off-licence and sub-post office in Cornwall. It was open many hours and I found it very restrictive. After getting it running smoothly and reasonably profitably it was unchallenging. So I took more and more time out to enjoy offshore sailing as a first mate with the Ocean Youth Club,

running a new small government Youth Training Scheme and, at the local Polytechnic, was a part-time small business tutor for ex-servicemen and women. Taking practical tests to become an Ocean Yachtsman, doing assignments to get a City & Guilds in Youth Training were no problem, I still struggled with my block for written examinations.

Erica never wanted to return to Africa although I was hankering to return overseas but not in the commercial field. I began to realise that I wanted to work in the newly emerging field of "development", but at 40 plus I was both ineligible and unqualified to access any regular university. There were no scholarships for over 40s so I would have to fund myself. Finally Ruskin College in Oxford conditionally accepted me, provided I first showed some social commitment to the "developing world".

I signed up with the VSO and was to go to South Sudan when another conflict re-erupted there. I was redirected to the small island country of Tuvalu in the South Pacific, difficult to find on any world map as it is virtually on the both the date time line and near the equator. I was to be a Small Business Advisor ostensibly to train local staff to run an office which was modelled on a development bank.

Just after arriving in Tuvalu I swallowed and nearly choked on a fish bone. After consuming vast quantities of strong salt water to induce vomiting, the one doctor was unable to remove it, so put me under anaesthetic. As I was recovering in a single ward looking out onto a palm fringed sparkling blue lagoon, a US Peace Corps nurse was holding my hand and talking softly in a deep southern drawl. I was disoriented, having only recently left the UK I wondered whether I was in heaven after being involved in some terminal horrendous motorway pile up. When the US Peace Corps later left her contract due to the perceived lack of proper medical evacuation facilities, this lovely nurse departed with only a plastic carrier bag. She said her mother told her to bring no souvenirs back, but she left heavily pregnant, probably the best souvenir of all! Her partner followed and they are now living happily in the US.

My work was to check the feasibility of small business loan applications and approve loans. Two million Australian dollars, probably "conscience money" for previously plundered phosphate deposits, had been donated to our office as seed capital and invested as collateral against our small business loans. The concept was basically brilliant and I admired the vision of its establishment. Our organisation could administer and run itself on the interest, in theory mercifully free of any outside influence. In practice we were not allowed to do that. The Australians would, unasked, donate us a photocopier, the New Zealanders, not to be outdone or lose influence, would then donate us an electric typewriter. Then, due to the climate, we would have to buy an air-conditioner so this equipment wouldn't deteriorate. Donors were effectively creating an evil cycle of dependence. How could I encourage these Tuvaluans to resist these proffered donations?

This island community had had no experience of currency until in 1943 the US military came to stage their attack against the Japanese occupying the northern Gilbert Islands group. To start or do "business" in a small sharing community which previously had little use for any currency and to whom the very concept of trading was alien, was some social leap. The office I was in was set up as a parastatal (half government half private) quango nominally under Tuvalu's Finance Ministry. This ministry had a secretary who was a UK civil servant accountant on his first Overseas Development Administration (now DfID) contract. He was a pretentious, rather pompous, self-styled Calvinist, which in itself was manageable. But that he was an arrogant bully was more difficult to accept. To me this was a recipe for disaster as his behaviour brought out my antagonism. He left early, unpopular with all and significantly there was no one at the airport to see him leave.

The island group where I was living has been immortalised in District Officer (DO) Arthur Grimble's "Pattern of Islands" when still called the Ellice Islands. (This island group was arbitrarily named because a passing ship's captain (Gilbert) had some luggage in his hold addressed to Captain Ellice). DO Grimble is still not too fondly remembered as the palangi who had all their dogs murdered. Palangi means white man, literally ghost, as we are seen to be without colour. An interesting concept in itself: if Africans are referred to as men of colour, then as whites are we men of no colour? Tuvalu was the land of "night creeping", when young lads, by prior arrangement, searched out their young girl fiends for assignations. Families slept on mats in their open sided pandanus (a palm leaf thatch) huts, mother and father side by side in the middle, girls alongside mother, and boys alongside father. So to make an assignation was quite some feat, yet Grimble was determined to put a stop to what he saw as immoral behaviour. He sent his local policemen out on night patrols, only for the family dogs to bark when the police arrived and give the alarm. Drastically Grimble had all the island dogs shot. He was subsequently posted to the Falkland Islands. In those days colonial civil servants had to make and pay their own passage from posting to posting. Probably he was a misunderstood or misreported civil servant as his aggrieved daughter later published a book in his mitigation or defence. In those colonial days both the Gilbert and Ellice islands together had three expatriates, the District Officer, a priest and a meteorologist. Yet in the 1980's the Tuvaluan Island group alone (nine islands, eight inhabited, total land area 10 square miles or 26 square kilometres) there were over 300 expatriate "experts", with an entire country population of barely 8,000.

Funafuti (translated as 'beautiful bananas'); the capital island of barely one square mile encompassed a vast 100 square mile lagoon. Parts of the island were literally the width of a track with the ocean one side and the lagoon the other. No part of the island was over five feet (one and half metres) high. Much of my free time was spent sailing a locally assembled Mirror dinghy. The sun was fierce and however well wrapped up, invariably my exposed knuckles would blister up with sun burn. Returning to my house early one afternoon to go sailing I looked for my locally made plastic sandals to protect me from the sharp coral - flip flops, T-shirt and a lava lava (wrap) was office rig. No houses were ever locked and eventually a youth came in carrying a sack of fish he'd just caught and wearing what looked like my sandals. I questioned this to which after some thought and with no irony he asked *"how many shoes can you wear at once?"*. I felt rather small, the more so when he stacked my fridge full with all the fish he'd caught. How petty and possessive I was. In time I learnt to accept that in their limited language there was no "my", only "our". A seductive view.

Few of our business loans were defaulted on as family pride dictated that money was to be repaid, despite many previous loans being at best ill advised. I was introduced to misguided development projects. Imposed, inappropriate, unsustainable and worse. Imported pigs became sunburnt and didn't like to eat coconuts, so special feed had to be imported. Bees were unable to fly in the heat so failed to produce honey. Once established, unsurprisingly, the bees became irremovable and crept around stinging people when disturbed. Electric-powered ice cream machines were imported with no power to run them. Fish farms were constructed that fed only seabirds. Goats were imported which consumed all new vegetation and needed too much of the scarce fresh water. Consultants and professed "expert" monitors visited. Often their fees far exceeded the total project cost. I learnt that consultants invariably plagiarised all our file notes to produce their own costly glossy reports as their own. We took the definition for expert as "ex", a has been, and "spurt", a drip under pressure.

It took over a month to tour all the eight inhabited islands in the group on the bucket tramp coaster MV Nivanga, collecting copra in exchange for salt, tobacco and other essentials. Each island stop was for a few days and the entire island community would put on endless sumptuous feasts, games, dancing and interminable meetings as time seemed to stand still. Their language was limited and they had only 14 letters in their alphabet. To stress any point it was endlessly repeated. One island in the group still managed without any currency. I felt it was inappropriate, if not impossible, to introduce any form of business and although my erstwhile untravelled Financial Secretary "boss" thought otherwise, my views prevailed. Like many expatriates he felt uncomfortable at leaving the capital.

I was once arrested by the local police for riding my Chinese "Flying Pigeon" fixed wheel bicycle "without any audible means of warning". I had lost the cap of my bicycle bell. I had to go to court and the judge fined me five Australian dollars, the currency in use. Protestations that a new bell was on order from New Zealand and would arrive in three months fell on deaf ears. The judge scoffed *"You palangis just can't manage can you? Get an empty beer can, cut off the top and put some old nails in – then you will have your audible warning."* Tuvalu had a prison for defaulters who were unable to pay their fines; it was a bamboo fenced compound. At day the prisoners came out and did gardening, largely unsupervised, at night they returned to their compound. After all there was nowhere to run.

Few people got sick on these islands but in the health centre there were two sections. One arrow pointed to "Western" another to "Local". After my experience with the fish bone, I opted for local. With a restricted diet I had bad boils and unpleasant tropical ulcers which no scarce antibiotics seem to relieve. I tried the local treatment and lay for hours on my stomach in a darkened thatched hut whilst a frangipani scented coconut oil was gently massaged into the offending boils and ulcers. I must have fallen asleep and on awakening they had all amazingly quite disappeared. Not a blemish.

In many ways Tuvalu defied description, a cross between paradise and a prison camp. It was an interesting educative interlude amongst this scattered isolated Polynesian island community. The people were so delightfully gentle, trusting and sharing. They were such a beautiful people, still largely untouched by, and naive to, the world as we knew it. Tuvaluans would do anything for you, but at the same time they would expect total reciprocation. It was easier just to go with the flow and let your life be organised by them. Yes they were being taken advantage of by that development school which "knows best what is good for them". Was I guilty by association? Uncomfortably, probably yes.

Leaving the South Pacific I'd picked up some bug, apparently through drinking too much toxic toddy (palm wine). I'd lost my tolerance for alcohol and was warned by the London Tropical Health & Diseases doctor to no longer drink alcohol. He reckoned I'd already consumed my life-time's quota! Since then I've never knowingly drunk a drop and I admit it's not something I really miss. When urged by family and friends to stop smoking I generally excuse myself that, having given up alcohol I should, at least, be left with my pipe.

Chapter 8 - Education - and some time with Operation Raleigh

To be finally accepted by Ruskin College, Oxford, as a Development student was pure joy. The irony that Ruskin was the Alma Mater of Sierra Leone's President Siaka Stevens was not lost on me. Many African and most Sierra Leone Trade Unionists have passed through Ruskin College. In the 1970s I had started a preliminary Open University course in Plymouth where the tutor had thoroughly belittled and demeaned all the class as uneducated dunces. At Ruskin my previous knowledge and experiences felt valued. We had enlightened Oxford University accredited tutors who inspired and encouraged us and I revelled in this luxury of pure study and research. Academically I did well in my first year, although finances were a constant strain and challenge. I had become a workers' club barman, and worked some afternoons in a sub-post office. I also applied for an indoor night security job at a hostel where I could study and ended up being their weekend chef. Cooking alone for over a hundred recovering ex-convicts, drug addicts and homeless street people in a modern residential Cyrenians' Centre - staffed largely by foreign students learning English - was physically demanding.

I was eligible for a student's discounted bus pass. An acne-challenged National Bus Company youth took my application, looked at me and declared I looked too old to be a student. That I thought he looked too young to be even a third year secondary school student, let alone have a paid job, I kept to myself. I got my pass.

Following a request through now Brigadier John Blashford-Snell, during the Ruskin College summer break I went with the youth adventure charity, Operation Raleigh to Indonesia as an unpaid volunteer deputy expedition leader. My expedition boss was the charismatic if unconventional Wandy Swales. With a bluff exterior he was essentially a sensitive man with a heart of gold, both a nightmare and inspiration to work with and for whom I soon developed the greatest respect and admiration. Wandy was a veritable Pied Piper, the youngsters would follow him anywhere. I was based in Jakarta with the expedition thousands of miles and two times zones east. The expedition was hosting hundreds of international and Indonesian youngsters accompanying world renowned scientists who were researching many aspects in both the oceans and vast tracts of mountainous rain forest, previously closed by the military for decades. Indonesia then was in essence a military state - with velvet civilian trimmings. All our radio transmissions were monitored by the police, which in its turn was an integral part of the military. One day my police minder who personally monitored my radio transmissions failed to turn up. He neither understood nor spoke much English but took a carbon copy of my transmission log away with him after every session. Apparently he had immobilised an unfamiliar vehicle blocking the police station entrance by removing the air from all its tyres. This was great initiative, but as the vehicle belonged to the newly appointed Station Commander who was not amused, my minder was imprisoned, "as a lesson". It was to be a few days before he was released and we were able to resume transmissions as he held the only transmitter key.

At an Indonesian press conference a local reporter asked *"Why had I come as what could I do better than any Indonesian?"* I had no answer and increasingly I have appreciated this deep question and I now always try to use this as a yardstick for myself before taking any overseas work. Is this my best use? Am I going for selfish reasons? Am I depriving a local person and their extended family of paid employment? Perhaps others who go overseas "to help" or "volunteer" should think about this. Is this their best use or, as is so often the case, are they going for personal, essentially selfish reasons? Sometimes the most real help we can be overseas is back at home, raising funds, awareness, working in a charity shop, doing administration or, for those who can, joining pressure groups and/or lobbying.

In Indonesia one of our staff photographers disappeared with a young "Venturer" in strange circumstances whilst climbing the isolated sacred Indonesian 3,027 metre mountain, Binaya, in Manusela National Park on Seram island where we were working. Locating, hiring and mobilising a search helicopter and coordinating with the Indonesian military over 2,000 miles to the east was just the sort of challenge I relished. To hire a civilian search helicopter large and fast enough, the company required a minimum cash deposit of US$ 20,000 paid to their Jakarta office. Jakarta is one of the few capital cities I like, noisy, vibrant and exciting; it never seemed to sleep. Walking out of a bank with a brief case stuffed full of cash to go to their offices seemed to merit a little caution so I took two hefty Indonesians with me. The photographer had broken every rule not only in our book but, arguably worse, he had deeply offended local customs. He had not reported to the local village chief and mountain custodian, nor had any customary offerings been made (red cloth was favoured). No one else knew of this trip and the young lad had joined him without anyone else's knowledge. Fortunately this lad was the far more experienced mountaineer. Compromising photos of some of the girls had been taken on the mountain and, although it may seem trite to us, the photographer had whistled, which was reportedly offensive to the mountain spirits. To compound his errors, his back pack was later found to contain illicit drugs, another absolute no no. All attempts to fly in a rescue and search helicopter were hampered by an unseasonal mist masking the mountain top. As the locals later said, the mountain spirits had been deeply offended. After many difficult days searching, finally local trackers with a crack military mountain Special Forces unit, located the now delirious youngster and stretchered him down to where the helicopter could reach and land. Having fallen hundreds of feet he was immobile and had survived by licking the morning dew from his cape, whilst apparently chatting to all his imaginary friends. He was covered in deep scratches and the rumour was he had been mauled by tigers, but there were no wild animals so far up this mountain. His wounds were crawling with maggots which apparently kept them uninfected. Days later, against my better judgement, fiercely overruled by the expedition medical doctor, and at great danger to the rescuers, the photographer's body, was recovered and repatriated to his obviously distraught, but highly critical parents. His much decomposed and rigid body was packed in fresh coffee grounds (to mask the stench) and, before transportation back to the UK; was re-sealed in an outer lead coffin. The logistics and bureaucracy of this were interminable, but the British Embassy were outstandingly supportive and cooperative every step of the way. On collecting the corpse from the airport I found it incongruous that we travelled through the packed Jakarta streets with the coffin in a black sealed van with a red flashing light and sirens. Throughout I was constantly accompanied by a smartly uniformed Captain from Military Intelligence who epitomized silent courtesy. The entire cost of this repatriation operation was over £50,000 - sufficient at that time to buy a substantial three bedroomed detached house in the UK. Personally I considered it an unjustifiable waste of resources. When I die, let me be buried or appropriately disposed of wherever I am, according to local customs and sensibilities.

After this incident I moved out of Jakarta east to Ambon to be closer to the expedition and spend more time in the field, where I am happiest. In the field I noticed our scientists used bright blue cloths to attract and collect their insect specimens, yet this is the same colour canvas that the United Nations issue in refugee camps in Africa for shelter. Surely the UNHCR can not deliberately issue blue canvas to refugee camps which attract insects, even mosquitoes?

Indonesia is a land of tens of thousands of islands connected by a number of ferry boats, many notoriously unsafe and often over loaded. I was attempting to hire one such large boat that was rumoured to be moored on an outlying small island. I had two Indonesians with me to help me check the papers, licences and count life jackets. It had taken us long time to get to the island and longer still to walk the ten miles or so to the bay on the other side of the island where the boat was moored. To check the boat out was the usual pantomime as the captain strung us along; attempting to get us to double count life-jackets was a common ploy. Soon it was dark. Foolishly we had left our rucksack and overnight bag at the port where we landed and I insisted that we walked back. Personally I prefer night walking; it is much cooler and quieter. My companions were reluctant and after a time stopped dead in perhaps more than one sense of the word. They were adamant, not a step further and we stayed the night in a rough shelter. The lads with me were literally up at dawn and ready for the off. On reaching the stop point of last night I saw there was a cemetery on both sides of the road. We all knew, but I said nothing; in any event these guys set such a pace that they made sure I needed all my breath just to keep up with them. It is so important to respect others' cultures and beliefs, however incomprehensible. Indonesia is such an attractive country with beautiful cultured and intelligent people. It was my incredible good fortune to climb Krakatoa (which last famously erupted in 1883 sending a tidal wave around the world) and other active volcanoes, visit the impressive 8th century Buddhist temple at Borobudur and spend a week in Bali visiting so many other fascinating places - I even went by public bus again. Near Krakatoa I watched a breath-taking display by youths from the nearby Badui isolated tribal group as they pierced themselves with swords, ate hot noodles cooked on live fires on their heads and, most incredibly to me, poured corrosive acid over their near naked bodies their clothes disintegrated but on their bodies there was, apparently no lasting effect. This was no illusion of light, the next morning we were all on the beach and swimming together, these young men's bodies were quite unblemished in any way. I was told it was mind over matter. With regret I missed a visit to the komodo dragons on Flores Island, something for another time.

All expeditions involved at least 200 people of all nationalities, abilities and ages, from brilliant scientists to US military personnel and youngsters from all spectrums of society. Every three month expedition had one month of intense dedicated activity of scientific research, a month of adventure and a month for community support projects, in areas which were often hundreds of miles apart. To coordinate all this, move the personnel and supply the logistics was exactly the sort of challenge I loved. I consider I am an able, practical and efficient administrator capable of hard work over protracted periods in difficult situations. I am quick to learn and adapt and have an ability to identify, communicate and motivate at all levels. The more difficult it became the more alive I was. How we change and slow down with increasing years; now I find I can cope simultaneously with one or two problems, three or more seem to get me rather flustered. Although rather in awe of our academics, something that has stayed with me throughout my life, I found some were a real delight and an encyclopaedia of fascinating knowledge, whereas others were a little precious and could be impractical and difficult to please. With a willing learner I can be a patient and tolerant teacher, happy to pass on my skills and experiences. Sadly not all expatriates overseas are like this, they can be jealous of their knowledge and, perhaps feeling insecure, reluctant to train others. I get a great personal joy and sense of satisfaction when those that I have trained can do my job and invariably surpass my achievements. I have been told that this is essentially my innate laziness to get others to do my work. So be it. I am more than happy to let others do things and make their mistakes, so long as they are not life-threatening or inordinately wasteful of resources. Making mistakes is an excellent, if not always the best, learning tool. No one of us will ever "manage" a situation the same way, but as long as our goals are the same, the results will be similar. I cannot abide those who are unable to admit to mistakes and always try to justify them or blame others. I have little tolerance for fools and less for pretentious poseurs. Perhaps only those who fund corrupt practices offend me more. But it takes two parties to perpetrate corruption, although in my view those who make the initial offer are arguably the most culpable. My behaviour in Sierra Leone continues to haunt me.

It was a delight to be in Indonesia. Apart from my expenses I had only been paid a modest amount for this expedition. As I had travelled around privately as a tourist, I had managed to save little and I was still relatively penniless. I deferred my return to Ruskin College for a year as I was offered to continue in a modestly paid deputy capacity for further expeditions in Indonesia and later Kenya. Based nearer the expedition area in the Moluccas, by chance on a Seram island quay-side, I was fortunate to meet Bing Tjiu, an English speaking high school graduate who became my interpreter, indispensable fixer and later companion. He was from a large part-Chinese family who were quite unaware that Bing spoke any English, let alone fluently; they had never considered his higher education. He was a minority Christian amongst nearly 180 million Muslim Indonesians. There was only one Christian University in this huge country. He spoke beautiful soft, unaccented English which, he claimed, he had learnt through the BBC World Service. I later lived with his family for some weeks in their crowded yet spotless small house and it is to this I owe my increased realisation that other cultures have so much to teach us. I helped him to attend the minority Christian University and years later, with some of his family, I attended his impressive graduation ceremony as a Batchelor of Economics. In a short time he was successfully managing a vibrant US sales company. Unrest sparked by hyper inflation and religiously-fermented riots destroyed many Christian homes and businesses and sadly this young man became lost to me from this time. Dear Bing had the double disadvantage of being Christian and, with a Chinese father, looking decidedly Chinese - a stigmatized race. How many families must have lost members in civil wars and riots whose situation remain forever not known. It is this not knowing that is so hard.

I moved from Indonesia to Kenya and we had a new military expedition leader, Colonel Mark Watts. As different from Wandy Swales as possible but great to work for and whom I highly respected. In Kenya I felt in my element, I knew the language and had retained many contacts, both in the Kenyan military and amongst some of the more enlightened expatriates who had stayed on. Better, I had helped draw up the budgets for these expeditions so felt more in control of expenses for what were to be three consecutive three month expeditions. Soon we rented a centrally located government bungalow with a very large compound. The Kenyan Army loaned us a fleet of trucks with drivers and, with the help of a volatile Italian, Sergio Beccaloni, we reconditioned a fleet of old Toyota Land Cruisers. A friend also loaned me her Range Rover, although I drove it little as it was felt a more suitably prestigious vehicle for Colonel Mark, with which I totally agreed.

Appearance and style can mean much in Africa. In rotation all our expedition participants climbed Mount Kenya, including a young disabled lad who, climbed unaided. On reaching the summit he seemed more worried about losing his disability allowance on his return to the UK, he had reason to worry. They went on camel treks, worked on community projects building schools and supported hosts of research scientists. We were able to bring my Indonesian translator Bing to take part in one of the Kenyan expeditions. This was a sort of "thank you" for his more than six months unpaid work for me. Bing, with a Chinese father, was denied Indonesian citizenship until he could apply on reaching 21 years. As a technically stateless person his travel to Kenya was not easy, but was facilitated superbly by the British Embassy in Jakarta, British Airways and the High Commission in Nairobi with his transit in London, probably not the most direct route. Few countries welcome stateless people, even as transit passengers. Both our overseas diplomats and British Airways get a great deal of often deserved criticism but when they are minded to help, doors can open like magic. We had youngsters travel without tickets or passports and the repatriation of bodies, never easy, was managed without fuss.

One Saturday the Range Rover was returned unexpectedly early after an emergency service; inadvertently Mark had sunk in a wadi (a dry river bed). The vehicle was not due back from the garage until Monday. It promised to be a quiet weekend and Mark was away. So on a whim it seemed a good idea for me to take it for a "test drive" and I took it north towards Nanyuki, the miles sped past and after some hours I had branched off on the road to Meru where a retired soldier friend had bought a small ten acre farm. Unsure of the off road track I passed what I thought was his farm, but was confused by the large number of parked cars and people around the house so drove on. The road petered out so I returned to ask where my friend's farm was, to be greeted by a priest who said they knew I was coming and were waiting. We all then trooped to a sheltered corner of a field where I could see an open grave and a small plain wooden coffin before it dawned on me that this was a burial. At that time I was helping my friend's second son Kenneth go to Primary School, had he died and was this his burial? Standing on the mound of freshly dug earth watching the small coffin clumsily fall into the grave, I was a mixture of emotions, when a small hand grasped mine and I looked down to see Kenneth's shy bright-eyed smile up at me. It was his elder brother who had died. Kenneth stuck to me like a shadow and, as it was a holiday time, came back to Nairobi with me for a few months. Kenneth later travelled with me to Zanzibar and Ethiopia before graduating with a diploma in tourism; he is now working in the Kenyan tourist industry. Why was I drawn to attend this funeral at this time when four hours earlier I had been sitting in our Nairobi office with absolutely no intention of travelling or knowledge of this funeral? To an African the answer is simple, *"God called you and we knew you would come"*. It is after all just a matter of faith.

Kenneth's father had been a boy soldier at Kenya's independence and so then was a relatively well educated person for that time. Finishing his army contract he had bought this small farm and we had kept in touch. Married and with three children in an era when country families were still huge, I had advised him to keep his family small. This was a mistake and, I now see, an unwarranted ignorant interference on my behalf. Their first child, daughter Mercy, was healthy and strong, but not too bright, their next son, Alex, had died so young (of a congenital heart problem) and, when eight year old Kenneth went away to boarding school, there was no one to herd the animals and help on the farm. They "took in" Jason, a young boy from a poor widow with a large family who lived nearby; effectively he became a part of their family as a surrogate son. Jason was loved, well fed, and clothed with all Kenneth's cast offs, given a small plot of land for himself and allowed to go to school for a few hours a day. The next time I visited, Jason had gone. A field worker from an international adoption agency had arrived on his motor cycle, taken his details and photograph and, within days, he was whisked away to a city orphanage paid for by his new 'international sponsor'. I was told that this is what always happens, once photographed, they're lost. Was this really the best for Jason? I doubt it. That the agency field workers are paid on a commission and expenses basis says something. Pardon my scepticism for international 'sponsor a child' schemes.

After two expeditions Colonel Mark was replaced by a rather inadequate children's social worker supported by an even more pompous, self-serving Army officer. His arrogance reminded me of one of the reasons I'd originally left the British Army. Our new leader was not easy to respect, least of which he referred to our youngsters as "kids", a term that does not endear itself to me. I realized there would be a serious personality clash and, ever penniless but proud, I resigned, but not before I had ensured with the Operation Raleigh Office in London that I could return after the expedition's end to assure employment for all our contracted Kenyan staff. In Kenya I was even banned from those very offices I'd rented and set up, which the security company guards I'd hired must have found distinctly embarrassing. I literally moved over the road to stay in the Nairobi Club and relax.

After Operation Raleigh finished in Kenya, getting jobs for all our local staff was relatively straightforward. They were superb staff, both skilled and, importantly, trustworthy. As I still knew many potential employers all were soon placed. One young store-keeper we'd employed chose not to accept a job offer with the Breweries, notably the best employer in Kenya, but to go to Art College. Steve, undoubtedly extremely talented, is now an eminently successful and a much sought after artist. At college his instructors were privately selling his work and I went to remonstrate at the college. The college Indian Principal was distinctly abusive in Swahili about me to Steve; I understood every word perfectly, but said nothing. Steve was so upset he refused to attend his graduation ceremony, although I later went to collect his Diploma. After graduation his father wanted him to get a "proper paid job" like his brothers, but after long discussions, Steve and I negotiated a year's trial for him. Within that year Steve, as an artist, was earning more in a month than any of his brothers in a year, so his father relented. During one of his art exhibitions, his self-built house, studio and everything he possessed was burnt down, most probably due to a self-wired electrical fault. *"How lucky"* he said *"that all my paintings were in the exhibition and I have sold enough to build a bigger better studio house"*. This indomitable positive spirit makes working with Africans so refreshingly rewarding. As this artist matured and his success grew, his gentle quiet attitude never changed. Whilst Steve is now well established, as "S Lance"; initially it was not an easy path for him to follow. Now he is in popular demand by upgrade tourist hotels to run "art workshops". I held an art exhibition for him in London at which all his works were successfully sold. Sadly due to the delaying bureaucracy of the UK consular visa service, he was unable to obtain his UK visa in time. Steve sincerely maintains that this is his God given talent to be used in His service.

This sincere and humbling attitude was one I would later experience constantly in Ethiopia. Helping both Bing and Steve to develop their abilities and talent to become confident, young, self-sufficient men with worthwhile careers beyond their wildest dreams, would go a long way to encourage me help others through education later.

My second year at Ruskin College passed quickly and without event. I found this time helpful in learning how to better marshal and express my thoughts and I loved reading about colonialism and imperialism. The popular conception of colonialism was that it was exploitative and "a bad thing". Sierra Leone, like India, had evolved from a trading company where the notion of the colony having to pay its own way and make a profit certainly prevailed until the end at independence. Yet there were good things: the average repatriated slave (the Creoles) could be assured of a better education in the 1830s than their counterparts in England. And in the 1850s professionally educated Creoles were filling posts such as the Mayor of Freetown, Surgeon-General and more. The UK built railways in many of its colonies, was this to control and exploit or to build an infrastructure? The dubious role of "missionaries" in their many guises was and is questionable. However well meaning, unless they have other needed professional, technical or teaching skills, I can find little to justify their presence, either historically or currently. In my experience Italian fathers were the best as most had practical "hands on" engineering skills.

From Ruskin I returned to Sierra Leone to write my dissertation. My subject was the importance of education as a pre-requisite for any development. In Freetown I was supported by the Honourable Minister Professor Dumbuya, an old University lecturer friend, recently appointed to the Ministry of Education, Culture and Sports. International bon viveur and excellent companion, he seemed out of his academic comfort zone in this Ministry. When the national football team lost, this highly educated and charismatic man maintained as a mitigating circumstance that he had been bewitched. Later further disgraced he and his wife were publicity humiliated and paraded naked through the city's main streets. He died shortly afterwards, reputedly of alcoholic poisoning, induced no doubt by shame. What another sad waste of resources.

On this visit Sierra Leone, normally so bright and colourful, had become a grey, drab and dismal place: there was no regular power or piped water, no fuel, little food and empty shops. Those few who were out on the streets seemed to drift aimlessly about without will or purpose, like zombies. Lack of fuel meant no cars and deserted streets; the town had an uneasy disturbing atmosphere. I stayed in the almost deserted Brookfields Hotel. There was no water but I found if I dismantled the bath taps and put an empty old paint can underneath, enough water dribbled out during the night to help me get by. The hotel had few resident guests although at night it was busy with ministerial Mercedes on lady "assignations". Food was very scarce. Breakfast as served was generally tea without milk or sugar and a hunk of bread. One day the waiter whispered that this morning he had some jam which he proudly presented. The waiter stood nearby and watched me eat, visibly salivating. Somehow I lost my appetite and told the waiter I'd had enough. He quickly cleared the table and, like a hamster, amazingly managed to stuff the remaining bread and jam in his mouth before he reached the kitchen door. The lad must have been ravenous; how difficult, almost cruel, to have to serve food when you're starving.

Returning to the UK on one of the last British Airways flights, our flight omitted its scheduled next stopover in neighbouring Liberia. The early civil war clouds were gathering and Monrovia airport was already insecure.

At Ruskin, I was still coping with my three part-time jobs of weekend cook, postal clerk and bartender to earn enough to get by. With some difficulty I managed to overcome my panic, fear and temporary amnesia during written examinations and left with an overall distinction.

I was accepted for a taught Masters degree in African history at the School of African and Oriental Studies in London, but it was quite beyond my financial resources so I chose to do an MPhil research degree in development at Swansea University. Swansea had promised me payment for post graduate tuition work to fund my living and study. In the event after a term's teaching this offer was rescinded with no payment and, also being recently divorced, I again found myself penniless and in need of paid work.

Staying in cold, bleak, damp lodgings in Swansea was reminiscent of my early days in Warrington. I sold what few of my possessions I could manage without yet was reduced to just existing and it was not easy. As a non-academic I felt out of place and unwelcome in this friendless place. Maybe this was just paranoia or my sense of inadequacy, perhaps I did little to help myself, or maybe I just didn't fit. I was proud but out of my depth.

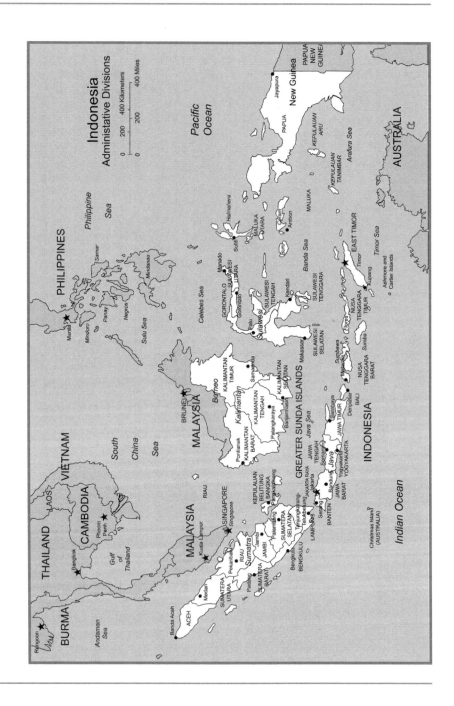

Meetings with President Siaka Stevens
of Sierra Leone - 1974

Erica and I with acting Soviet
Ambassador to Sierra Leone - 1973

British Council
performance of
"My Three
Angels" - 1974

With Italian Chairman Dottore Franco Rivoira and Percy Johnson meeting Italian Consul's wife

With Erica and Chairman of Standard Bank of Sierra Leone

With Erica, Percy Johnson and his brother, Deputy Governor of the Bank of Sierra Leone

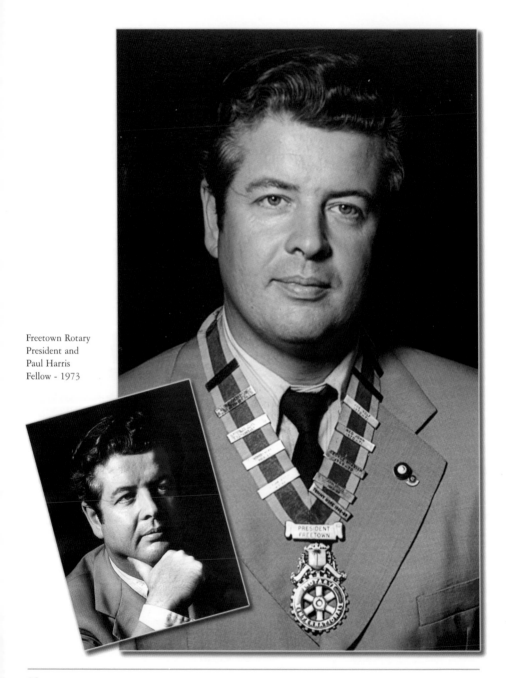

Freetown Rotary
President and
Paul Harris
Fellow - 1973

Sailing on
Funafuti Lagoon,
Tuvalu - 1984

Operation Raleigh Indonesia - 1987
on Seram Island ferry

Operation Raleigh Indonesia - 1987

Visit by Duke
of Gloucester

With local staff and volunteers

Operation Raleigh Indonesia - 1987
with interpreter Bing Tjiu

Field radio communications - with my police "minder"

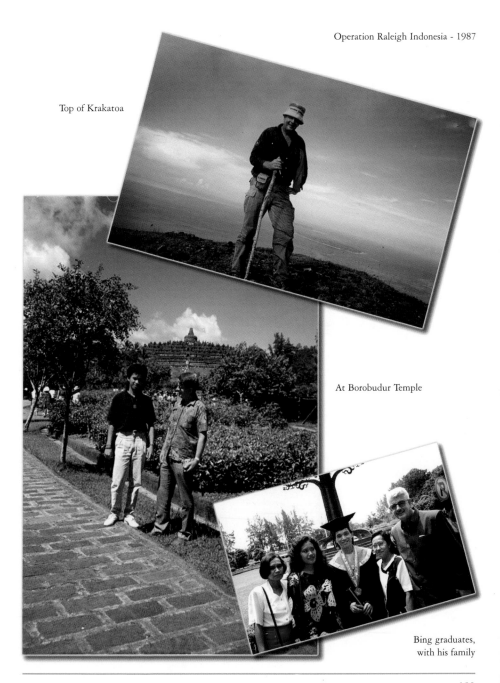

Top of Krakatoa

At Borobudur Temple

Bing graduates,
with his family

Operation Raleigh Kenya - 1988
Indonesian Bing Tjiu joins us

Operation Raleigh Kenya - 1988

Kenyan
Equator

Nairobi National Headquarters

Operation Raleigh Kenya
- 1988

Nairobi HQ
Communication centre

Field visit

Visiting (Retired)
Colonel Syuma and
family on their farm

Chapter 9 - First "development" jobs - Afghanistan to Somalia

I got two overseas job offers, both paying peanuts. One was in a Sri Lankan refugee camp and the other in Afghanistan, which the Soviets had recently left. Refugee camps are soulless places. Refugees are displaced and disoriented, often just fed to be fed again. They are places of inactivity and boredom as the refugees wait until they can return home. Boredom can lead to mischief, trouble and worse. Running refugee camps is unrewarding with little sense of job satisfaction. I prefer to try to help those already at or near their homes, so I chose an organization working primarily in agricultural rehabilitation and development in Afghanistan.

It is not uncommon for small but successful organizations when in receipt of massive and perhaps unexpected injections of funds to grow beyond the skills and experience of their committed founding members, as I can only surmise had happened here. The management's lack of vision and flexibility was frustrating, as was their rather patronising attitude towards the Afghans which I found difficult to accept.

My job title was rather grand as Deputy Director (Research and Training) but the pay less than I was receiving 10 years ago in Sierra Leone. Big titles often mask miserable remuneration but, now over 50, I could not be too choosy and it was a step in the direction I wanted to go. I had learnt that in all bad experiences there are generally positive outcomes that can lead to something better. My first job was to run an "Away" senior staff training weekend in the Chitral valley of North West Pakistan. I selected an old palace converted to a hotel which was many hours travel away from our office. We were a few expatriates, our Punjabi accountant and twenty Afghans, all male of course. Academic development theoreticians our London office may have been, but they seemed disconnected with the realities on the ground, and certainly on any sort of personal level with the Afghans. I thought little of the presentational abilities of our London office, but on a prosaic level it was a moderately successful weekend and certainly a good bonding exercise. One of our expatriate ladies complained to me of her inability to sleep the night before due to a howling dog in the hotel compound. Unthinkingly I mentioned this to the Hotel Manager. Minutes later I heard a shot ring out. *"Good sleeping now"* the ever obliging Manager proudly told me, *"dog dead"*. In future I would have to be a little more circumspect as to what I said and to whom.

During the Soviet occupation of Afghanistan this charity had grown fat with generous ODA funding. This was probably on the back of their providing military intelligence to our diplomatic military attaches, often garnered by enthusiastic but inexperienced back-packing "Hooray Henry" world travelling adventurers. When I was with them they were still struggling to make that transition to a professional, development oriented organisation, something I now note that happily they have since seem to have achieved. It was the classic case of an organization having grown too quickly without the necessary professional leadership and infrastructure. The in situ leaders lacked vision and seemed averse to either change or advice. The Afghans for their part, were absolutely charming, highly intelligent, independently minded and with a delightful sense of humour. The organisation was undoubtedly hostage to most of them and their whims as the Afghans managed to run circles round us all. I found those Afghans working with me to be solicitous and utterly loyal, even if sometimes this could be transient.

Early on I was a naïve idealist, quite altruistic and I failed to see aid or development as the big business that I now appreciate it really is. Western country aid is often accepted more for its spin offs, look at the failed anarchic state of Somalia. Internal or national interference, with justifiable reason, is discouraged. As far as possible we should keep military peace-keeping initiatives far removed from development aid, and the military should stick to peace keeping and not become involved in development aid, of which they have little experience. Mixing the military support and humanitarian aid confuses the population, and often those implementing it. The military are not adept at humanitarian aid, no more than would any charity or NGO be good at peace keeping. I have seen some appallingly inept and inappropriate military aid executed; such as un-requested schools built in soon to be vacated camp areas far from any habitation.

My knowledge and background helps me to work and approach developmental support differently and with a better perspective. If we are to help develop anywhere, as a first premise we should surely be invited and welcome, above all we must be able to identify and empathise with the people. Admittedly our local staff could be self-serving (why not?), devious and were adept at manipulating to their advantage us "franks" (foreigners); more specifically in our case by their running guns in and poppy resin out using the void spaces under the stretchers in our cross-border ambulances. It was my extreme folly to have been seen to be too aware of these activities. Today's loyal companion was most certainly a spy for someone, and everyone had their price. To define friend or enemy in an Afghan concept was always confusing. I thought then how sensible it was that there were no overseas or UN troops involved in Afghanistan. Admittedly that was pre-Taliban. Little cognisance has been taken of Afghanistan's history. The Afghans decidedly defeated an entire British Army in the late 19th century and the entire might of the Soviet military machine later, so one wonders at the wisdom of our current political peace-keeping venture made on the premise of keeping the Western world safer where *"not a shot would be fired"*.

Before the Soviet military backed administration totally failed, the only way we, as an organization, could get our inputs to our Afghanistan project areas was on mule trains over the mountain passes. This was officially discouraged by the Pakistan authorities, but they had little direct control over this tribal area, so to cross the border the Afghans became experts in deception, setting up many decoy crossing attempts to confuse and cover the real party's crossing. Crossing from France through the Euro tunnel to the UK must be like child's play to most Afghans. During the winter snows, the mountain route was closed for at least five months, so if you were in and the pass closed due to early snows, there you stayed for the duration. Our hired mule trains, often of over 500 animals, mainly carried seeds, fertilizer and flat-packed gabions over these passes. The mule train master was paid half on leaving and his agent received the other half on arriving at the given destination for safe and full delivery. That war lords could seize the mule convoy at any point, discard our goods to load up with their missiles and land mines, was an acceptable risk we had to take. Mules that faltered or became sick on route were abandoned, to die. Some of our mule trains arrived, some didn't.

Among my research and training responsibilities was training computer operators. Women were not trained, as this was prohibited in our lease as being far too modern and sensitive! Throughout my entire contract I never saw any woman's face, although I carried on many long and deep conversations by phone, through shutters or closed metal gates. Never confident or fully computer literate myself I was informally taught here by a bright incredibly patient Afghan; he'd never been to any school but could competently teach any computer programme, simultaneously in the three languages we used. One day he confided in me that he liked me because I was always smelly. I asked him to repeat or explain better. *"Your face,"* he said, *"it's always so smelly."* We later agreed he meant smiley.

Most of our Afghan staff were young but unmarried and had a great infectious capacity for life. For them certainly life was for living to the hilt and off duty they were fun to be with. We seemed to have lots of long weekends and around our Christmas time I went with a group to the hill station at Murree, just outside Islamabad. It had snowed and was incredibly beautiful, just like a UK Christmas card scene, even the buildings and firs were reminiscent of England. An even more exciting long weekend was when we all went to Lahore for a kite flying weekend. The sky was filled with brightly decorated kites flown from flat roof tops and the event was taken very seriously, kite strings even had razors to "cut" your opponents' kites down. We had left our vehicle at Peshawar airport and paid for two days parking, but on our return the vehicle had disappeared. Eventually traced to the police HQ; apparently for security reasons no vehicles were allowed to be parked overnight at the airport. I spent a day drinking tea and exchanging pleasantries with senior police inspectors until the vehicle was released. They explained they suspected it had a bomb in it and were quite intransigent about not releasing it until a "fine" was paid. That smashing the windows and removing it clumsily by fork-lift truck may have detonated any bomb seemed of no concern to them. But it had been a terrific weekend, memorable now in many ways.

We ran a UNHCR funded tailoring unit making school uniforms for refugees. These shawal kamize's (a long shirt and baggy trouser suit) effectively doubled as their every day wear; few children had any other clothes. Our tailors were supposedly war disabled. Land-mine disabilities had elevated the status of previously ostracised polio victims or other amputees and I had allowed them to join this programme. Wars had prevented the distribution of polio vaccine so surely any polio victim is as much a victim of war? The myopic UNHCR inspectors ruled otherwise and, with a pettiness that I was to become used to, withdrew our funding and we had to stop our programme. We had often recommended and arranged replacement prosthetics from the Geneva-based International Committee of the Red Cross for those who had lost limbs. After fitting these were sometimes traded in their obvious desperation for much needed cash, food or goods and the amputees returned, with different identity papers, to try to get a re-issue.

Flying into Kabul's embattled airport was scary, as the ancient Soviet Antonov cargo planes we got lifts in spiralled down in a fast dive, shooting off missile deflectors. As a pilot my knowing how to throw a plane into spin did not make this manoeuvre any easier to sit through as a passenger. After landing we often taxied past randomly scattered, still smouldering plane hulks. Clearing airport formalities through differing militia groups was uncertain and nerve racking. Yet the alternative of driving overland back to Pakistan by small bus was no less fraught. By bus we continually stopped for periodic prayers and thanksgiving after every successfully avoided rocket attack, negotiated road block or ambush. At every stop I was obliged to get off the bus as some women might have remained seated inside. My fellow bus passengers could barely conceal their unhappiness towards me as they correctly perceived I was a potential problem and cause of additional delays. Afghans have a pale complexion and after a few weeks in the UK and in jeans and T-shirt they can easily pass as a white European. It didn't work the other way round and although I was wearing the local shawal kamize, turban and had a fuzzy excuse for a beard, for a long bus journey or on close interrogation with poor language skills, I still couldn't "pass" easily as an Afghan. I had to travel alone because we passed through so many differently held areas, no Afghan partner would be acceptable and able to pass through all areas. At the Pakistan Khyber Pass border the bus almost managed to leave without me. Only persistence, desperation and some luck allowed me to relocate and re-board the bus. It had an Afghan carpet on the roof that I was bringing as a wedding gift for my nephew, Richard. At this London wedding I intended to wear a traditional Afghan cream embroidered wedding outfit with plumed turban, but I got the distinct impression the family would not be well pleased and a morning suit was hired for me. Attending the wedding luncheon I sat at a table with a number of bright young city bankers, they and their pretty partners were scanning the room. With their puzzled looks they whispered *"Where is Richard's eccentric uncle?"* I kept very quiet.

After years of Soviet occupation Kabul was incredibly still unscathed; it was a beautiful ancient city boasting some incredibly elegant ancient architecture and surrounded by snow capped mountains. For a time I was the only frank staying in the Kabul Hilton, also untouched, shops open and tea ceremonies continuing. It seemed a veritable haven even after their Soviet appointed President Najibullah had been publicly hanged on a lamp post. The hotel swimming pool was empty, but I was told this was so even during the Soviet occupation. Unbelievably the Hilton still accepted American Express and I was billed in US dollars. My fellow guests were hundreds of the Commander Masood's, the "Lion of Panjshir"; smart, well disciplined quiet troops. We all ate together in the large dining room. In the streets, car showrooms still had their plate glass intact with luxury foreign cars, generally Mercedes, on display. This was so unlike the aftermath of any coup or leadership shift in Africa. Bright, clean, white tiled, ice cream parlours flourished and some restaurants were open. Hungry urchins would clear your table the minute you paused eating for too long. There is nothing quite as incongruous as an ice cream parlour packed with full-bearded and turbaned mujaheddin fighters propping up their AK47s and delicately eating the wonderful Afghan pistachio topped ice creams in long fluted glasses. When these public places suddenly emptied it was a good indicator that an attack was imminent, and it was advisable to head for the nearest cellar! The zoo still had a few animals, there was certainly one resident lion left I saw, and the parks were full of the most beautiful strongly scented roses. After rocket and mortar attacks on the city, body parts were bagged and the clear up was swift and matter of fact. Most poignant I found were abandoned children's toys and their little shoes. I imagined this would have been similar to the London blitz. Markets soon re-opened, trolleybuses ran, cinemas and music shops were open and thriving, but again this was pre-Taliban.

Internationally admired and deeply respected by most Afghans, Commander Ahmed Shah Masood's inspirational leadership had repulsed over nine Soviet attacks into the Panjshir valley and was quoted *"We will never be a pawn in someone else's game, we will always be Afghans"*. Whilst serving as Defence Minister he was assassinated in 2001 by two posing as a Middle Eastern TV crew, cameraman and interviewer; their camera was an adapted silenced pistol. This was certainly a variation on the normal media assassination by words. After his death Masood was a Nobel Peace Prize nominee. His death was a great loss to the country. Afghanistan is a country divided by the Pashto and Dari languages composed of equally passionate Shia and Sunni Muslims - it will never be easy to unite. The only thing that seems to unite Afghans is their ability to fight so as repulse "intrusive" foreigners. Will we never learn?

At an attempted lynching in Kabul by one of the many feuding militia groups, my diplomatic visa meant little, but my one-eyed giant of a non-English speaking driver stubbornly stood by me. His loyalty was impressive and humbling, as with so many Afghans designated to "look after me". In the autonomous, but generally lawless, Chitral region of North West Pakistan we were again ambushed and attacked and, for my own safety, this same driver managed to get me arrested by the police "for my own safety". A rich US young "adventurer" had apparently disappeared in this area without trace a few months previously. In my police cell, although unshackled, I noted that the new leg and arm manacles concreted into the wall were made in Birmingham. Was this UK's only remaining manufacturing industry, apart that is from the tens of thousands of "agricultural" machetes the UK exported to Rwanda just before their genocide? I wondered whether the export of shackles was eligible for the British Government export guarantee scheme. I later leant that the correct terminology was "restraints", or is this a US term?

On release from my police cell, as I had lost and had rearranged a number of my teeth in the ambush, I attended a tented Afghan field dental clinic that we passed. They were both charming and solicitous, getting out a large picture book on dental treatment. It was laid out rather like a Grade One ABC with on one page a large colour picture opposite a single simple sentence of instruction. They could not read English and I was a poor translator. They bound my mouth up and gave me some pain killers; it was to be five days before I reached our base, surviving on soup sipped through a straw. Having lost most of my teeth in that ambush, after collecting my kit from our Kabul house, I returned to the UK for dental treatment. There was little sympathy from our UK Director and I was paid off after signing a disclaimer against making any claim for medical or other expenses from the charity.

I had never looked for or courted danger and always took local advice, but this did not seem enough. Development was fast becoming an industry, with bright young graduates rushing around the world's trouble spots "saving" the needy. In these conflict zones, the brightest locals, businessmen and politicians were quick to turn this "aid" to their advantage, not necessarily to those in need of support. Both donors and receivers had an inherent need to prolong any conflict and neither to turn off this tap of funds and materials pouring into their areas. Idealists who asked too many questions or were perceived to "rock the boat" in any way were not welcome. As one Afghan succinctly put it, *"this aid is donated to help Afghanistan, we're Afghans so why all this bureaucracy of project proposals, implementation plans, monitoring and evaluation, why not just give it to us, we know what to do and how to do it, that's helping Afghanistan?"* They had a good point. I had begun to realize that I was, as dubbed, at heart more of an "Africa man". I did not return to Afghanistan and took a post as Relief Team Leader in Somalia.

So I was back in Africa - to an anarchic situation that still gives me sweating nightmares.

I was working for a US relief outfit. Prudently all their US staff stayed safely in Kenya, yet we non-US staff were often openly criticised to our faces as untrained incompetents. For US$ 100 a day we hired vehicles previously stolen from us and other aid organizations, now run as a business by gun toting youths, yet we still provided the fuel. Their guns were protecting "their" vehicles, not us. I was used to Afghans stealing our generally new vehicles, but at least they were subtle enough not to try to hire them back to us. From our base in Badhere as Team Leader I was overseeing some food distribution in an area which had recently changed war lords, but was no less peaceful as the "new" man obviously needed to build up his reserve stocks. Our relief food was flown in from Kenya, some even using those "temporary" border airstrips I had built so many years ago. The German aircrews were superb, the US alarmingly casual and the British stiff, superior and distinctly uncooperative. Aircraft left their motors running and at the slightest sign of disturbance or gunfire would take off, cargo doors still open and whether offloading had been completed or not. Burst landing tyres were incredibly changed within minutes. When there was no rain, at peak times the airstrip could handle 12 aircraft daily, each bringing in about 10 tons of food. I admit to barely any food distribution plan other than to try to flood the market and hope that some of the food would filter down to those in greatest need. Gradually markets began to reappear and previously silent, wide eyed children began squealing and playing again. Child deaths dropped from over 100 to less than 30 daily; perhaps on a small scale we were doing something worthwhile. We tried to work with a nascent civilian administration but those designated personnel seemed to change daily.

A charismatic, smooth talking US diplomat, ostensibly from their Kenyan embassy, always seemed to be involved with Somali chiefs or war lords, was he their puppet-master? But in this surreal world no one was ever quite what they seemed. The more I stayed, the more confusing it became. Some were loosely attached to the World Food Programme (WFP), we had our share of religious zealots, mainly from the US, freelance aid junkies and a rash of embarrassingly inexperienced unprofessional "MONGOS" (My Own NGO – mainly it seems funded by US small communities who collected funds to come and "do good works"); these ad hoc groups abounded. What was their agenda? As ours was a US aid agency based in Nairobi, US "officials" visited regularly, although few stayed overnight and it was unclear what their status was or what they represented or were officials of. These visitors compromised any neutrality we had and I saw this as a distinct disadvantage. This would become much more so after the mighty US military machine arrived with their staged flood-lit beach landing, looking later like something from a movie. Reputedly this scene was re-staged and shot more than once, but probably in the circumstances, re-shot is an unfortunate turn of phrase. Again the fighters buried guns came out and Somalia once more became an open shooting gallery.

After some weeks a US Special Forces reconnaissance team flew in early to Badhere. They were five, ostensibly civilian, a white, a black, a Filipino, a Chinese and a mixed race, driving their new unmarked Isuzu trooper. Unasked, uninvited and, to me, distinctly unwelcome, they stayed overnight in our compound, totally comprising any aid neutrality we might have fooled ourselves as having. I may have been called "Team Leader" but in reality I had little or no authority. The next morning their Isuzu failed to start so we lent them a battery as I was more than anxious to see them leave. We had tried to warn them of land-mines and suggested they take our "mine clearer" with them; after all he had originally laid them. It seemed only minutes before the tell-tale pop and puff of dark smoke heralded their misfortune. Long before we arrived locals had stripped the vehicle of anything recyclable. After an hour a ship-based US helicopter flew in to take what remained of their bodies away. We never got our new battery back. It was to be a long month before the main body of the US military made it the hundred miles or so from the capital to where we were. Already the long serving local Imam and his young daughter had been shot dead on his mosque steps for refusing to fly an anti US banner. The US military were mainly young and black, what you could see of them under their huge helmets. Whoever briefed them? They really thought that they were coming to save and free their black brothers. Giving out candy and big hugs as the Somalis picked their pockets, stole their guns, walkie-talkies, sun glasses and then seized and drove away their huge Humvees (a sort of large jeep). Too soon the US military lost their "arrogant world saviour role" and turned very bitter, revengeful and nasty. The US was involved in a conflict which few could understand but which could never be militarily "won". There are few winners in any war, only the politicians and arms dealers.

With the US military came the international media, always clamouring for that award-winning clip or sound bite. With the media came the celebrities and visiting us, in his element, was the gun lobby king Charlton Heston - who even brought his own preferred brand of peanut butter. CNN flew their vast crew in a Hercules cargo plane with enough bottled water even for showering. Most international media felt that we, the aid fraternity, were there and in a job because of their world wide promotion of this disaster and accordingly behaved as if "we owed them". Some expected us to feed and accommodate them overnight from our minimal hard won airlifted resources. Those who fouled our overcrowded overused latrines were the least popular. A BBC reporter had driven from Mogadishu in a rented Range Rover and when it arrived in Badhere the local gun boys re-claimed it as stolen from them. He was without transport and seemed more than dismayed that we were not able to either provide him with another vehicle or recover his Range Rover, we were not Hertz. Not a happy man, and this was certainly not his finest hour compared to his cool decisive on-screen TV personality I was accustomed to. There are always stars that memorably shine in any muck pile and exceptionally I commend two superb reporters from the Toronto Star to whom I will always feel indebted. They saw a problem and stepped in, often unasked, whether it was manning the radio or helping tally our stock returns. I hope they got the best inside stories, they certainly deserved to. One fraught night whilst they were with us a camel spider (we called it that as it was camel coloured) was in our sleeping quarters. The male would anaesthetise you whilst asleep, and the female then ate your flesh. One US marine fell off his cot bed to wake up with half his face missing - it is not the best insect to have around. Scorpions are a mere irritant by comparison.

But If the international media behaved appallingly, we aid agencies were little better. Cooperation? Forget it; this was fighting for that sound bite to get the biggest share of a gullible international donor's dollar. If that meant slagging off the opposition or worse, so be it. A dirty war on all fronts.

In a few months more of my room-mates died than in all my active military service. In my room the adjoining two camp cots were often unfilled by evening. In our neighbouring Red Cross compound, a young Swiss accountant, surrounded and guarded by the US military, was murdered for failing to hand over the keys to their dollar strong boxes quickly enough. Sensibly we only dealt in the less attractive local currency which we "counted" in cartons by weight. Physically counting these vast bundles was neither feasible nor medically safe. In these situations currency carried a myriad of transmittable diseases. The Somalis were quick learners and have now graduated to the really big time as they ransome ships for millions of dollars.

Inter warlord rivalries driven by greed and power-lust flourished, dissidents were locked by fellow Somalis in shipping containers and left to suffocate in the intense heat and de-hydrate, generally to death. Effectively we looked away, as we did to blatant corruption, grand theft to order and more. No item was too big to get "re-located". We excused ourselves by not interfering in local policies and whilst this may have been pragmatic, it made me feel distinctly uncomfortable. We were paying a local "mine clearer" for every mine he brought in - he had laid them so generally he knew where to collect them. Amazingly he was then allowed to dispose of the mines himself - unsupervised. It was a fantastic money spinner as he brought back the same mines day after day, I started noting their serial numbers and when I attempted to curb this practice I became an unpopular target. With my military service I respected land mines and arranged their disposal myself. In a few days I became mysteriously ill and was flown out in a coma. How could I have been so foolish?

The routine of packing my bag every morning and leaving that farewell disposal note on top was wearisome. I need not have bothered, when I came to in a Nairobi hospital a few days later my bag had been looted of my few personal items of any value, a short-wave radio and camera! When discharged the doctors just shrugged and wrote "Somalia virus" on my papers.

After recovery as I was waiting in our Mogadishu compound for a new position. Sky News phoned on our satellite link for a "sound bite". *"It sounds too quiet"* the interviewer commented, *"no street battles?"* It was a Friday and everyone was at the mosque. Sky

News rang off, it was not dramatic enough. They should have called earlier when I was sheltering on our compound patio during a particularly explosive extended street battle - always an uneven contest, the US always lost. Unsurprisingly the Somalis knew their back streets far better. The Somalis also had enough stolen walkie-talkies not only to control their fighters on one wavelength but also to mislead the US forces on their main US battle net.

There are those who maintain that humans are naturally aggressive and predisposed to be predatory. Sir Wilfred Thesinger was one who claimed to prove this from his time living with the Afar and Marsh Arabs. When we met in a very English-furnished Nairobi bungalow, I was seeking his advice on hiring camels; he was wearing a rough hairy tweed almost orange thick suit as we sipped our Earl Grey tea from huge willow pattern cups. Thesinger was of another era and meeting him was like entering another time. He was born in 1910 in the British Legation, now Embassy, in Addis Abeba. He was an anti-authoritarian and intrepid explorer/adventurer whom, despite his many critics, I greatly admired. Thesinger still had the presence to get away with the most outrageous and non-politically correct actions and comments. In the 1930s he had ditched a fellow traveller as he couldn't stand his socks and, sharing a tent with other explorers in the Hindu Kush referred to them as poofters as they had the temerity to use a thin mattress. The one thing I disagreed with Thesinger on was his belief that all mankind was naturally aggressive. I believe that people are naturally kind, compassionate and supportive of each other, with only the situation or environment making us evil towards each other. Simplistically if we smile we get a smile back; if we are kind, kindness is returned. We are all good or have good in us and increasingly I have tried to bring out this best in those I met and worked with, sadly not always with the success I would hope for.

Much time spent in war or conflict zones both in the army, on refugee or development work is, of necessity, spent waiting during extended periods of inactivity. A good book is recommended, as it is portable and no power is needed, but reading is not always easy. One day I was playing dominoes with our Somali agriculturalists, professionally qualified from UK's Cirencester Agricultural College. I felt sad, I could always leave, and they could not. This was their home and there seemed so little future for them or their country. Finally I was happy to be sent as a dispatcher out of Mombasa Airport until my contract ended; a quiet safe logistic post. Doing little good, hostage to all, unwelcome and unsafe, I was unwilling to become another forgotten statistic. Again it was time to move on; no one, certainly no expatriate, could be proud of their role in Somalia.

Chapter 10 - Ethiopia with the Red Cross

For many decades Ethiopia had not had a good press. Haile Selassie, as Ras Tafari, Regent of Ethiopia had visited England in 1924 following Ethiopia's acceptance as a member of the League of Nations the previous year. He had also spent 1936 to 1941 in exile in Bath and was generally revered in England, but with his assassination in 1975 and Ethiopia's close allegiance with Soviet Russia and subsequent famines, Ethiopia, was not thought well of in the Western bloc. Emperor Haile Selassie (meaning Holy Trinity) took this royal title in 1931 following various subterfuges to dethrone Dejatch (Prince) Eyasu who some would maintain was the rightful contender to the throne. Emperor Haile Selassie claimed direct descent from King Solomon and is indeed still deeply revered by the Rastafarians (derived from his earlier given name Ras (Duke) Tafari) as the embodiment of God. Haile Selassie was a skilful manipulator and beyond doubt proved that he was born to rule. But however feudal the system that he inherited and continued in many ways to perpetuate, he was a moderniser who saw the need for and promoted education. This was to prove to his later detriment when those students he had sent to the US for higher education became frustrated on their return at the slow pace of reform and rebelled. From 1974 Ethiopia became known for the first of its internationally known "biblical famines" caused through a combination of droughts and deliberate policies of migration, systematic denuding of large areas, bombing and violent armed civil repression. Never colonised, little was known by the outside world of its rich history and culture. Still less of the unfortunate episode when Britain's military might, led by General Robert Napier, sailed in 1867 from India and marched hundreds of miles against Emperor Tewodros II in Magdala Fort. Lord Napier was a military engineer and I remembered well his huge full length portrait hanging in The Royal Engineers HQ Mess in Chatham, undoubtedly much a hero of his time.

Tewodros could certainly be a difficult if not despotic Emperor and given to violence, yet he was essentially a visionary and desperate to modernize his country. He wrote many times to Queen Victoria, whom he saw as the great Christian Empress, requesting support for modernization, but it is doubtful if Prime Minister Palmerston ever passed these requests on in full. On parliamentary advice, the Queen sent Tewodros a presentation pair of duelling pistols. Feeling ignored and to gain attention, Tewodros detained some assorted British adventurers, explorers, claimed missionaries and diplomatic emissaries. Tewodros certainly got more attention than he bargained for and in 1868, surrounded by the massed forces of British military might from India, he attempted to surrender to Napier. This was not accepted but before he would let himself be captured and Magdala looted, Tewodros shot himself, ironically with one of Queen Victoria's presentation pistols. He left a note to Queen Victoria professing his continuing love and admiration and bequeathing her his most precious possession, his son and heir, Dejatch Alemayehu to her.

It is long hidden murky story, where ultimately Dejatch Alemayehu became a favoured member of the British royal household, reputedly much loved by the Queen. Educated like most princes at the Royal Military Academy at Sandhurst, she later denied Dejatch Alemayehu permission to take part in any active service. Very well educated, extremely intelligent but understandably lonely and home-sick, Alemayehu kept requesting to be allowed to return to Abyssinia as its rightful new ruler. The Anglo-French Suez Canal had just opened in 1869 and at that time Abyssinia claimed sovereignty over Yemen. One needs little imagination to understand the consternation of the British Government to a highly intelligent English educated, military trained Abyssinian Prince returning to rule the two countries spanning the entrance to the newly opened Suez Canal. So how could Dejatch Alemayehu die in Kirkstall, Leeds, when only 19 years old? Take your pick of the many conspiracy theories. Victorian Leeds must have been depressing enough place, in the 1950s it was bleak enough, but to fall asleep in an outside privy and die of pneumonia is possibly the least imaginative. Queen Victoria was devastated, *"so sad to die alone".* As a testament to Queen Victoria's love, Dejatch Alemayehu is the only non-British Royal person to be buried in Saint George's Chapel, Windsor. Ethiopia, land of so much little known history, how could I not be fascinated to be posted there?

For decades flying across Africa was only possible, then as now, by the well managed Ethiopian Airlines (established with great foresight by Emperor Haile Selassie in the 1930s), so I had often passed through their bleak, unwelcoming, militarily run, Soviet-style, concrete edifice of Addis Abeba airport. The Federation of Red Cross and Red Crescent Societies had offered me a field delegate position in Afar, a newly created region of Ethiopia, and I hesitatingly accepted the minimum six month contract as the best option I had on offer. That over 20 years later I am still there should say it all. At 50 plus I was older than the usual field delegates and I am ever grateful to my paymasters, the British Red Cross, in what was essentially a young person's world, to have that faith in my ability and employ me. Hopefully I was not becoming too much of an intolerant crusty old cynic. My Red Cross country briefing was in Geneva. Another travesty of misinformation given by earnest, fresh-faced, barely travelled young graduates droning on with well meaning but often hilariously inappropriate advice. To be personally briefed by someone who has never visited, let alone worked overseas, is not always helpful. I was issued with a pack of strawberry condoms and my fellow delegate, married to an African, the chocolate ones. Was this racial stereotyping by condom? Of many country briefings, this one was memorably incongruous as I was advised to take rubber boots, thermal underwear and an umbrella. I was posted to the Afar Danakil Depression where it rarely, if ever, rains and, if lucky, night temperatures fall to blood heat after days shimmering at over 50°C in the shade - if you could ever find any. In the Afar region the recommended umbrella provided excellent shelter from the sun but I never knew what became of my thermal underwear and Wellington rubber boots. I was billeted in a converted shipping container left behind by the departing Soviets; it was certainly not the coolest place. The container conversion had hatches cut in the side as "windows". Our base was near the place where "Lucy", the oldest known humanoid skeleton at that time, was discovered in 1974. Lucy was then, at over three million years, the oldest known humanoid skeleton. Nicknamed Lucy after the popular Beatles 1967 song "Lucy in the sky with diamonds", the skeleton, now in the Addis Abeba museum, is in fact of a male. Since then other much older skeletal remains have been found in Afar - a place where bubbling volcanic sands could swallow a camel in minutes and where the scalding hot ground water had to be left out to cool before washing or taking a shower.

Africans are crazy about football; many can relate every player's name, their position and their score record in their favourite clubs, with Manchester United and Arsenal high on the list. To have a football team in Africa is a superb bonding exercise. Give them their own strip and you have created an instant cohesive, almost fighting unit. Rather like the British Old Pals Regiments that joined up to fight in the First World War. Later in the Sierra Leone civil war football teams had actually become fighting units, retaining their team names. Football with the Afar was always exciting. Predictably unpredictable, if in only how many minutes we could manage without a shoot out, and not with the football. Rules changed, sometimes footwear was allowed, sometimes not. This depended on the referee and how he saw the advantage to the side he favoured. Rather like a form of cricket played in the Pacific, any number could play and matches rarely ended without a pitched battle should we foolishly allow our team to score more than the Afar. That way both teams could abandon the game and claim equal victory honours. To the Afar to "play the game" is a totally misguided British concept, to play for them was to win, decisively. But after the Somalis, the Afar people were just a lovely, proud and dignified ethnic group and, more by default than design, my Red Cross contract was extended for a further six months. Certainly some of my highland staff felt, with reason, intimidated by the Afar, and after an altercation with some excitable Afar youths, one storekeeper did lose an ear. I felt I was always treated with a distant sort of respect, perhaps in fact largely ignored by the Afar as being generally irrelevant, perhaps they were right. After all they had seen so many ferengis come and go. The myth, perpetrated by the Ethiopian born explorer Sir Wilfred Thesinger, of the Afar wearing necklaces made from the dried genitals of their captured enemies was exaggerated. That I not only survived but thrived after a year with the Afar and remained relatively sane and sober was an apparent cause for wonder. An earlier delegate had not returned from local leave and the previous one, from the United States, nicknamed "Ato Ouzo" (Mr Vodka), had left in handcuffs and spent months drying out in a Frankfurt US Military Hospital. As some sort of recognition or thank you the Red Cross unusually permitted me to choose my next region to work in.

Following an earlier visit on my way to visit the ancient capital city of Axum, I had been overwhelmed with caring kindness in Tigray, so I chose to go to Mekelle, their regional capital. Here my life changed forever as described more fully in the following chapters. I have since come to proudly regard Tigray as my second home and the incredible Tigreans as a people I feel both humbled and privileged to be identified with.

When I arrived, Ethiopia was awakening from an 18 year nightmare of civil war, particularly the "Red Terror" gangs who murdered indiscriminately and openly in the capital. Mekelle had been severely bombed and had even endured a week with no sun due to smoldering smoke clouds. Repression, torture, forced mass migrations; starvation, and deprivation, physical, mental, personal and property destruction had left many shattered people in a destroyed land. In 1984 Michael Buerk had referred to it on BBC TV as *"a disaster of biblical proportions"*. An estimated one million died and many more were displaced. To find words to adequately describe my emotions, I have not found easy. I met youngsters growing up with absent fathers, born to young girls raped by soldiers. So many "grandmothers", often in reality raped and shamed mothers. One remaining child found alive in the ruins, following the entire destruction of Hawzien village, was eventually brought to me for support. Many still daily pass those places where friends died on their way to school during bombings. So many youngsters grew up malnourished on meagre rations and had had no childhood, no games, no fun; that they are now so mature, well-balanced and strong is a source of continual wonder to me, but more of that later.

Axum was fascinating, the ancient capital of what is sometimes referred to as the Land of Punt, which long pre-dated Abyssinia. It is the reputed home to the jealousy guarded legendary Ark of the Covenant and location of many burial stelae over two millennia old. But it was Lalibela, hidden deep in the central highland Lasta Hills that totally captivated me. Due to near non-existent roads at that time it took me three separate attempts driving across and often up rocky dry river beds to reach Lalibela. I was one of the first wheeled vehicles to reach Lalibela since the fall of the Derg Marxist government. It was already dark and enveloped in a thick damp cloud when I arrived. After the Danakil depression this was distinctly damp and cold and added to the surreal "other world" atmosphere. I was met by a young man, Solomon Gebayew, with the words, *"Tomorrow I am your guide"*. Solomon lent me his warm thick cotton gabi (shawl) and said he would call at 5 am to show me the churches. Shivering and damp, I slept little and was more than ready to leave before dawn to visit this labyrinth of rock-hewn churches - still a continual source of wonderment to me every time I visit annually as a sort of pilgrimage..

Reputedly built by only a few masons in the 11th Century, I expressed disbelief, *"An impossible feat of engineering"* I said. *"The trouble with you Westerners,"* I was rebuked by Solomon my guide, now a successful hotel entrepreneur and as my "soul brother" much more than a friend, *"is that you have no faith, of course at night hundreds of angels came to help"*. Now with that sort of faith, anything is possible.

Jews have lived in Abyssinia since well before Christ and the country became officially Christian when King Ezana converted in the early 4th Century. His early coins bore a crescent, later the cross. Ezana had been converted to Christianity by two Syrian shipwrecked slaves Frumentas and Adiemus, who King Ezana had taken in and they had become prominent members of his court, one eventually became the first Patriarch of the Ethiopian Orthodox Church. So Abyssinia was a Christian country whilst much of Europe was still running around painted with woad and wearing animal skins. It could never attract those missionary zealots with the excuse of converting the heathen or bringing light to the "Dark Continent". The Jesuits tried in the 14th Century, but did not stay long. To this day Ethiopians are fiercely and rightly protective of their Church, its beliefs and customs.

Ethiopia has never been colonised in the accepted sense. The 1884/85 Berlin "Scramble for Africa" Conference carved up Africa to suit colonising powers, with scant regard for ethnic boundaries and realities on the ground. Italy was allocated Eritrea and the southern part of Somaliland, but it had always coveted Abyssinia and invaded in 1895. This resulted in a resounding defeat of the Italians at the Battle of Adwa in 1896, the only European army to have been defeated by an African army. The Italians never forgave this and Mussolini planned a retaliatory invasion by the early 1930s. Despite Emperor Haile Selassie's impassioned, measured and articulate appeal to the fellow members of the League of Nations, to the eternal shame of those member nations he was ignored. Mussolini, revenging Italy's shame at their 1896 defeat, was allowed to invade while the world looked away. Here is not the place to catalogue the atrocities, the aerial mustard gas attacks, the machine gunning and bombing of the recently formed Ethiopian Red Cross Society (ERCS) and their attached international medical staff, nor the plundering of ancient relics. Every Ethiopian knows this history whilst we in the West can feign ignorance. The Italians stayed but never ruled. The Second World War started, from which the Italians eventually withdrew as the British took over the administration of Ethiopia from the occupying Italians. But the Italian legacy was not all bad and the Ethiopians bear little ill will; they built some good roads and some buildings of outstanding both classical and art deco architecture. Many Ethiopians learnt Italian and took to pasta and ice cream and the country had been enriched by their presence. But the Italians never colonised Ethiopia in any sense of the word. Many Italians stayed on and intermarried and today older Ethiopians will still greet me in Italian. Perhaps surprisingly there is no animosity towards Italy or the Italians and in 1996 it was to stage an on-location centenary re-enactment of the Battle of Adwa. I was asked to play the part of the defeated Italian General Oreste Baratieri. My Red Cross partner, himself a recently demobilised freedom fighter, cautioned me against it; any battle re-enactment could well escalate as the Ethiopian participants became over enthusiastic. I knew what he meant: in Sierra Leone I had taken a part in a BBC dramatised documentary of Stanley meeting Livingstone and knew how African "extras" could easily get carried away. Happily the re-enactment did not take place and was replaced by a historical seminar. Intriguingly when terrorists take over control of a country or government the terminology changes and they become freedom fighters or liberators.

When a new Red Cross delegate arrived in the country as I became the longest serving, I was often asked to show them around, a sort of orientation and induction. This generally meant a week or ten days slog around most of our current projects, generally over very rough roads. One delegate came in the most superb tailored, colour coordinated kit with zips and pockets everywhere, topped with a stylish bush hat. This may have been suitable for an exclusive Kenyan safari but looked distinctively over the top where we were. Despite the roads, vehicles generally had a twenty year life span, although they became increasingly unreliable. Most of our vehicles were from the 1984 famine period or before. Delayed by a faulty thermostat we were late arriving in one town and had little choice where to stay. We had to have a room with an obligatory secure walled compound for our car. We were too late for any food and the rooms were basic with a small alcove to serve as both shower and latrine. The cost was one birr, then about 20 US cents. Outside the room was a bucket of muddy river water for shower and/or latrine use. I awoke to hear my fellow new delegate loudly remonstrating about his bill of three birr, the equivalent of 60 US cents. In Ethiopia it is not thought good manners to raise your voice, something I admit I am not always very good at myself. He had used a bucket of water in the evening and one in the morning, but these cost one birr each. That in addition to his salary he would have been drawing a per diem equivalent to well over 100 dollars (then 500 birr) for every night out of the capital, whatever he spent seemed to have slipped his mind. Much later he applied to return as Head of Delegation but was not appointed. Ethiopians have long memories.

There were other confusions about money. In Government hotels we expatriates then had to pay in US dollars at a fixed rate of five birr for one US dollar. Checking out of an Addis Abeba hotel and paying a bill one morning to catch an early flight (most local flights tend to take off at 6 am) proffering dollars, the pretty receptionist said what I thought was "I'll give you sex". I was aware that there had been a certain amount of relaxation of the strict Derg rules on morality, but it was surprising to be offered this service at 4 am and I must have looked puzzled. "Sex," she said, "sex dollars to the birr, not five." Confusion thankfully over with relief, or should that be without relief!

My time in the field with the local Red Cross, overseeing the building of micro earth dams, health centres, terracing hill-sides and planting trees, all by the community with food provided through the Red Cross for work, taught me much. As an Engineer I would have never believed it possible to build an earth stone-faced dam with no machinery and only 7,000 people with head pans, donkeys and determination, but they did it. We supplied wheel barrows, but surprisingly with their usual African poise, they never seemed to master balancing the one wheel, or maybe the terrain was just too rough? Their organizational ability was breath taking and I marvelled not only at that but the hard work put in by the essentially subsistence farm workers, 70% of whom were women, many with babies strapped to their backs. So many men had been lost during their civil war. That the food ration they got for this back breaking work was barely equivalent to 2,000 calories a day was scandalous. I continually battled with those in authority in Addis Abeba for our rightful allocation of supplies, but to many in the capital Tigreans were still perceived as the "enemy", sadly something that to some extant persists to this day in some quarters. During the Marxist regime the Red Cross had the monopoly on all international aid. Many HQ staff had illicitly acquired "concrete" houses, vehicles, food and drugs on these exclusive corrupt contracts and perhaps were finding it difficult to accept that these fat times were over. During my time, more than a thousand tonnes of Danish Red Cross donated drugs "disappeared" from the central pharmacy warehouse over two nights, quite a considerable logistical achievement which must have utilised the entire Red Cross transport fleet. Apart from a hapless security guard, no one was ever apprehended; immediately and unquestioningly the Danes re-stocked the warehouse.

Travelling internally was still not easy, roads were not always safe, as remnants of the disbanded Derg military set up ambushes, and they were often in an appalling condition from indiscriminate use by Derg military tracked vehicles. Rather than the long gruelling two day drive north I was once tempted to fly and on that occasion had to report on four consecutive days to the airport before our plane finally turned up. Apparently it had been forced to land elsewhere, and ran out of fuel which had to be trucked in overland. Hours or even a day's delay and/or cancellation were usual, but a four day wait was my record. Better perhaps than the Kenyan Airways plane which taxied for take-off, only to return to the apron as a warning light indicated an outside door was not closed. After an hour or so swarming with technicians whilst we sweated inside we were finally apparently ready to take off. The pilot announced the problem was fixed as they had disconnected the warning light; nothing about fixing the faulty door. Travelling in developing countries was all about arriving safely.

After some years in Ethiopia as now the longest serving delegate I reluctantly had come to the capital to head the overseas international delegation. I had never thought of myself as a head office person and was generally happier to be in the field or in the background as a "Number Two" in any organisation. Perhaps I asked too many questions or began to show too much interest in what I should not because it soon became apparent that by some I was perceived as a threat and a dangerous man. After I made what I thought was a moderate low-key speech to a team of international donors decrying corrupt practices, my desktop PC was wiped and my personal laptop disappeared; all from within the supposedly secure Red Cross HQ compound. My British Red Cross International Director was not sympathetic and said I'd shot myself in both feet. He was correct and ultimately my residency permit was not renewed and I had to return to the UK. The international delegation office was subsequently downgraded and now lacks any executive status.

Some time in West Tanzania followed, overseeing three refugee camps for Zairians, Burundians and Rwandans. Each camp was in a triangle 50 kilometres apart to stop any interaction and continuation of their disputes. No refugee was allowed to stray more than five kilometres from their camp boundary on pain of arrest or being shot by the Tanzanian paramilitary. Generally these para-militaries were more likely to shoot first and ask for an ID later.

We were based in the western most part of Tanzania at Kigoma near Ujiji where in 1871 the New York Herald's adventurous investigative journalist Henry Morton Stanley famously "found" missionary and Doctor David Livingstone - a part I had played in for an earlier BBC documentary drama series filmed decades before in Sierra Leone. Our main refugee camp for Zairians was basic and sited in an uninhabitable malarial swamp that no one would or could normally inhabit and survive. Decades previously some Danish agriculturalists had tried to farm it and they all had died from malaria prematurely. We were allocated to this site because the camp UNHCR had previously constructed was later deemed by the Tanzanian authorities to be too near a national park. They feared not only countryside degradation, but loss of animals. They were right: fifty thousand scavenging refugees can quickly denude a land as effectively as any swarm of locusts. Before we are tempted to think how kind and humanitarian of the Tanzanian government to allow such an influx of refugees, let me not sound too cynical to point out that this UNHCR refugee operation was a very big money earner with unlimited both legitimate and illegitimate trading opportunities. International "aid" can be a very lucrative business in disaster areas.

In this Lugufu camp to start with there was no safe drinking water and no sanitation, yet refugees were pouring in at 5,000 a day. After liaison with the Kigoma military commissioner (my time in the Kenyan Army helped me get an interview with this normally distant and autocratic Colonel) my halting rather rusty Swahili managed to get him to hold this influx in Kigoma town for about ten days. This would allow us to better prepare the camp infrastructure. Getting the first refugees to dig latrines was not easy. In any civil crisis the early refugees are typically the educated and rich, unaccustomed to personally do any physical labour. Our camp ground was swampy and a few feet down was the water level. We had yet to install a piped water supply and all the water bowsers were elsewhere - of that, more later. As the Zairian refugees poured in I heard that there was great consternation in Europe as a boat with 400 Albanian refugees was attempting to land in Italy, but the Italian government claimed it was unable to cope with such an influx. At its peak Lugufu Camp held nearly half a million refugees; by 2010 this figure had fallen to a little under 100,000. The world knew nothing of our camps or situation; thankfully for once we were then off limits to any media.

Nominally head of this sub delegation we had a German Red Cross Medical Team in our camp. Their leader was a rather imperious doctor/surgeon who insisted on operating quite independently. Were there shades here of resurgent German East African colonialism, the rulers of this country prior to the First World War? One of their doctors contracted malaria, but their expert medical team refused to medically evacuate him which I strongly recommended from previous experience with this falciparum malaria. Sadly within days he had died on our local airstrip with the flying air doctor team after they had belatedly agreed to medivac him.

The Germans regularly rotated the members of their medical team; new staff changed over at the local airstrip and after a long flight invariably jumped in their left hand drive vehicle, to drive the fifty odd kilometres to Lugufu Camp. The Germans refused to use those Tanzanian drivers allocated to their standard right hand drive vehicles. Tanzania still drives on the left of the road, as in the UK - but not as in Germany. In the bush one invariably drives in the centre of the road until meeting the very occasional oncoming vehicle. On an encounter with an oncoming truck inevitably the truck went correctly to his left and the tired German driver's automatic reaction was to go to his right. They collided head on. As so often happens following a road accident in Africa the truck driver disappeared into the bush and was never seen again. We were there within a short time and had to extract four body parts from the totally concertinaed mangled metal remains of the Land Cruiser. I helped extract the dead and dying from the vehicle to be later roundly castigated by the Red Cross Geneva-based nurse for not wearing gloves and exposing myself to HIV risks. Gloves are not entirely practical in a 30 degree, high humidity, environment. In any event medical gloves would have been useless and torn to shreds by the metal shards. Subsequently my HIV tests were negative. I believe that this German team bore a heavy responsibility for these needless and tragic deaths, yet as Sub-Delegation Head, they were laid at my door. I had no recourse. As we built schools and a health clinic, which helped to stem the level of deaths from malaria and cholera, understandably the outlying local population complained that our refugee camp facilities were better than theirs. We were subsequently obliged by the Tanzanian government to build and service schools and clinics outside our camp perimeter for them. Power with responsibility I can manage and relish, responsibility without power or resources is more difficult to cope with.

Blame apportioned I was logistically and administratively sidelined by the Red Cross Head Office in Geneva, who had sent me few of the requested support staff. Our water distribution was also severely restricted by all our water bowsers (tankers) having been previously sent to Rwanda prior to my arrival which, understandably, the Rwandan government refused to return. This mindless insupportable short-term decision was made by an egotistical, Geneva based, self-styled, power crazed, logistics expert. I had crossed swords with this petty self-promoting delusional guy in Ethiopia. When he later visited Tanzania and, in a crowded KIgoma hotel bar, loudly proclaimed that my position was beyond my capacity I, usually the most peaceable guy, had to be physically restrained by our lovely Finnish doctor.

I left the Red Cross nearing 60, pride intact, although self-confidence a little bruised. When things go monumentally wrong the top hierarchy generally need a fall guy to blame. I just wasn't smart or political enough to avoid this. Visiting Geneva for a later de-briefing, I was made to feel that that I had leprosy or had been passed the black spot. I have never been one to pass or apportion blame and am quite prepared to admit to mistakes or deficiencies on my part or that are my responsibility. Perhaps this was not the most illustrious end to my paid career in Africa. It was uncomfortable at the time, but now I consider it both sad and faintly amusing. I certainly was not the first, nor would I be the last.

Chapter 11 - UK and A-CET

With that obvious wisdom that comes retrospectively, to have left the Red Cross at that time of my life was the best thing that happened to me. It forced me to look to myself, my strengths and my weaknesses, what I enjoyed and what I found tiresome. I was back in the UK with no income, no room or place to call my own and a few years to wait for my state pension. What could I do, what needed to be done, what was I good at and enjoyed doing? To be in this situation certainly helped me focus my mind.

I accepted a residential caretaker position with a religious organization but, for various reasons, the job became stressful for me. I found it difficult to accept my situation and I was constantly exhausted. My misery was compounded one early evening, returning from a Nigerian dance show in town, when I was mugged and beaten up within sight of my flat. I had survived Kabul, Mogadishu, Jakarta and Nairobi unscathed but, just after a heart operation, to be attacked in the UK was difficult to accept. But a heart operation or being mugged was apparently no excuse not to work.

After four years I was finally both physically and mentally beaten, although I couldn't realize it or admit it to myself at the time. I had become depressed but I thought depression was for wimps, all I needed to do was "buck up and sort myself out". I classed depression as some sort of mental inadequacy or excuse for laziness and it is not something that I found easy to share with people. Sometimes you need to experience something to really know and understand it. This was one of these times and I then knew how wrong I was. I was fortunate to have some friends who helped me. Words can destroy a person and it is too easy to make people feel utterly wretched and useless. It was a personally deeply upsetting and destructive time, sleepless, sweating nights, feelings of inadequacy and exhaustion. Increasingly I almost lost the will to live. I had coped with post traumatic stress disorder during and following my times overseas, but then the Red Cross had an excellent professional counselling service as part of its de-briefing. I seemed unable or ill-equipped to manage myself through this. Finally one afternoon cutting the lawns, I collapsed in the street. The motor mower traversed the road, fortunately missing all the traffic. The good Samaritans who came to my support were a Chinese student and an elderly lady with a walking frame, interestingly both from rather marginalised sections of the community. One of them must have called an ambulance and I was taken to hospital. I thought I was strong, but I was beaten, physically and mentally. My doctor signed me off as sick for a few months.

Few knew the depths of how badly down I felt and probably I didn't even realize this myself until much later. This is my first time to write about it, let alone talk about it much to anyone and it has not been easy. But good things always come out of bad and I made some very kind and understanding friends whose support and patience has been both my joy and privilege. Friends' support is invaluable, not necessarily to say or even do anything, but just to listen and be there. Hopefully I have become more understanding and appreciative of those I now know are depressed. Pills, potions or even therapy can't lift a depression, in the end it is only in you. It was A-CET that filled my life and gave me that strength and sense of purpose to literally start living positively again. Many years later a dedicated supporter, on receiving an A-CET Award of Appreciation at a ceremony in Ethiopia, during her acceptance speech said that after her husband had died some years ago her life was empty and without purpose for some years. *"Then I found A-CET,"* she said, *"and my life changed."* I understood.

I had lost my job and the residential flat so I needed somewhere to live. You need great fortitude and single-minded determination to visit any council or government benefit office. Previous encounters on behalf of struggling youth trainees had prepared me to be bullish and determined, but for myself it was different and more difficult. I never have had any personal sense of my "rights or entitlements" believing that anything I got I had to earn or work for. In those public government offices toilets are invariably locked because I was told that we, the public, *"despoiled them"*. I had been similarly reprimanded when I reported a public telephone out of order: *"It's you public who are to blame"* the irate operator blasted me with. So in the council housing office, in front of hundreds of pram wheeling mothers who surely had greater need of toilet visits than I, one was forced to publicly request the key and then a security person was loudly summoned to personally accompany and supervise me. So the choice was either an uncomfortable bladder or a debasing public humiliation. When my appointment finally came I went into a cubicle for my interviewer to tell me *"You have purposely caused yourself to be dismissed and thereby homeless so you are not entitled for council housing".* I felt devastated and in my utter helplessness, I saw red and went moderately ballistic. Despite her armoured plate glass screen, she visibly backed away and told me *"Don't get angry with me".* "OK," I replied, *"get someone I can get angry with".* Minutes passed and I saw eyes peering through their back door spy glass at this troublesome applicant. Finally a lovely, obviously high caste, Indian lady came in, personally greeted me and said I would get a flat vacancy notice tomorrow. We knew each other as, when I was caretaker, I had previously arranged bookings for her Islamic Professional Ladies Group. So it was not so much what you know or are entitled to, but who you know. She was as good as her word.

When I returned to the UK in late 1997 on advice I had received from family and friends, notably Gerald Wingate, I founded and registered the small charity African Children's Educational Trust (A-CET). My sister Ruth provided some modest seed capital and a firm of pro-bono lawyers to get it all formalized. Wally Rabey, a retired banker friend from 1965 with decades of experience with the Standard Bank in Africa, became a Trustee and our Secretary, and our Examining Accountant was my friend Michael, the Auditor whom I had met in 1970 in Sierra Leone.

After well over ten years A-CET, in its small way, now has an enviable reputation for providing high quality, easily accessible rural community elementary school facilities for thousands of Ethiopian farmers' children with modest long-term scholarships for hundreds more. Some are completing their PhDs or MBAs in the UK. Well over 100 of our ex-students - including Ethiopian famine survivor and now Graduate Nurse Birhan Woldu (who came to international fame as the 1984 famine survivor on Sir Bob Geldof's Live Eight Concert in London's Hyde Park in 2005 and the Oprah Winfrey Show in 2004) - are now all gainfully employed or self-employed in worthwhile, often key positions, where they are contributing to the development not only of themselves but also their families and their country. Yet in 1997 A-CET did not exist; so how and why did this happen?

Much of my life in Africa seems to have been dictated by coincidences and this one started on my way to visit the ancient capital and stelae (pillar-like monuments) at Axum, North Ethiopia in 1993. What we may term as fate or coincidence is not generally accepted in Africa. It is God's will and I believe that. Thirsty, we had stopped for a bottle of water in a small shop on the way. It being the first day of the Ethiopian month (Ethiopia uses the Julian calendar of 13 months) we were invited to drink coffee. A traditional Ethiopian coffee ceremony can take hours when you are properly obliged to drink three separate brews. It is thought lucky if a stranger joins the group and it seemed discourteous to leave early; in any event Ethiopian home brewed coffee is superb and too good to pass up. As a result our onward journey was seriously delayed and on leaving it was near dusk. As it was not allowed to drive after dark, we diverted to the next city, Mekelle. Stopping at the first hotel of only two at that time, the Green Hotel, I was approached by a smart young man who after the usual courtesies, offered to take me out for a traditional evening meal. At this time there was little food to be had, there were few restaurants or cafés and the hotel did not serve meals. Meals were available if you knew where to go, served by some matronly ladies in the equivalent of their "front rooms". The meal I was offered was "tolu", a sort of peppery stew fondue with simmering dried meat strips bubbling over a small charcoal burner – it is eaten with rolled balls of barley paste dipped in it using local wooden forks. I fear my pathetic description of this tasty speciality may well have some Tigreans crying with horror. Like so much Ethiopian food, it is quite unique, spicy and above all filling. This young man was Bisrat Mesfin and with that meeting, both our lives changed forever.

After my year with the Afar the Red Cross offered me a new posting. Knowing nowhere else in Ethiopia from the many places then offered and available, and after the cheerful open hospitality I had received from Bisrat, I chose Tigray. Bisrat was then a Grade 11 secondary school student. He is now the Manager, and much more, of the local charity Ethiopian Youth Educational Support (EYES), the national implementing partner for A-CET. Later I learnt that no other Red Cross delegate was happy to go to the Tigray Region, wrongly perceived as a dangerous hotbed and centre of those wild terrorists - anti-government rebels now, as victors, renamed freedom fighters. Following their overthrow of the Marxist Derg they were now the country's de facto new rulers. This feeling by the Tigreans against the previous Derg regime was fully reciprocated and no representatives, however remotely thought to have been connected to the previous regime, were welcome in Tigray. In practice they were actively and not too subtly discouraged. Ethiopians are very proud of the country, and its history is well remembered. These Tigreans were the descendants of that only African army who had defeated the colonizing Italian Army at the Battle of Adwa on 1 March 1896. Such was this respect, tinged with fear of Tigray and the Tigreans; that for most of my time there were only two expatriate "aid" workers in Mekelle, the other being Danielle from the WFP with whom I had worked in Kabul.

At that time, Mekelle, the regional capital city was a shell of pock marked, battle scarred buildings, broken windows, few shops with little stock, no asphalt roads or street lights - but populated by the infectious enthusiasm of a cheerful, uncomplaining dignified and stoic people, all working hard to rebuild their city and their lives. Electricity and piped water had already been restored within months, something that in Sierra Leone following their civil war, had taken years.

Whilst working with the local Ethiopian Red Cross Society I had rented a modest house near the bus station. I spent most of my week living in the field helping to monitor and oversee food for work distribution programmes. The work element was building earth dams by thousands of still desperately hungry subsistence farmers. It was physically tiring but extremely fulfilling work and I convinced myself of its worthiness. Roads were difficult and not all buried land mines had been accounted for. We regularly had to replace my aging vehicle's shock absorbers, springs and tyres, although these were not always available, but with a good driver and African ingenuity we managed. Travelling after dark was unwise and discouraged, so I often had to sleep out. I stayed in the Genet Hotel, Genet means heaven. The beds were clean and cheap. After some months they "gave" me one of their sons, another Bisrat, to be educated in the city and I then became a part of their family, of 14 children. Even to this day I have been unable to pay for anything. They had a farm and mother Mileta's food was magnificent, almost as overpowering and wonderful as their love and friendship they unhesitatingly bestowed on me. Friendships in Ethiopia are for life.

In Mekelle a number of often abandoned, distinctly underfed, poorly clothed youngsters gravitated towards my house. I fed them, clothed them and helped them to stay on or return to school. Clothes were cast offs brought from my family and friends in the UK, no clothes shops were open or had any stock. The youngsters staying with me were soon looking smart and had great pride in their appearance, although local visitors criticized me for being scruffy, maybe subconsciously this was my Bob Geldof look and wanting to blend in. Truth was I cared little for what I wore so long as it was serviceable. Decades later people I'd worked with came up to me and greeted or introduced me, *"I knew you"* they said *"because you've still wearing the same shirt/jacket"*. As more important visitors came I became a little more camera conscious and invested in a suit. Soon in my house a rather dark, windowless, store was converted to a dormitory and, with the help of bunk beds and I managed to squeeze in up to eight of them. Their only "rule" was to look after themselves and attend regular full-time education. For this they needed no encouragement. At weekends a treat was to watch a video, usually an English classic loaned from the British Council. Two hour films often took three hours to screen as I explained the dialogue. Films featuring youngsters like David Copperfield, Great Expectations or Oliver Twist were great favourites. They could probably well identify with the story lines and characters. There were no language schools, indeed no private schools, in Mekelle then, yet all of these youngsters have since grown up writing and speaking articulately the most beautiful unaccented and expressive English. Treats were porridge and big bowls of custard - both brought from the UK as not locally available. My attempts to make ice cream were not so successful.

Tammy's story. Living near the bus station the dusty road outside my house was always bustling with activity from dawn to dusk. Youths gravitated towards the place ever hopeful of carrying travellers' bags or perhaps relieving weary unsuspecting travellers of some unguarded item. These were the bus station boys, an even sharper type of street boy. The bus station was locked at dusk and these boys usually slept under the parked buses for the warmth of the exhausts. Some who overslept had sadly met with an unfortunate grisly end as the bus moved off in the morning. I had to walk past the bus station on my way to the nearby Red Cross office and soon a scruffy little urchin would pop out from nowhere "Father, father carry bag". Initially I was more than reluctant to trust my brief case so we walked together to the office, both gripping my brief case. We must have looked an odd pair and after some days of this pantomime I relented and let Tammy carry my case. Later he produced an almost bristle free shoe-brush so that on arrival at the office my shoes, now covered with a thin film of fine dust, could be ostentatiously brushed off. I gave him enough cents for a tea and bombalino (doughnut) for breakfast. This was eight year old Tammy, turned out by his mother as old enough to manage himself so that she could better feed her many other children by as many now deceased fathers. Tammy was quick to make himself useful and helped Ferdie my Red Cross driver clean the car whilst tirelessly made himself generally indispensable around the house and compound. He was given some better clothes and was fed from the house until eventually he became a part of the household, but the rule was he had to go to school. He had always maintained he was Grade 3 although in fact, like so many before and since, he had answered the question with an answer to please rather than the truth. Newly enrolled at Grade 1 he soon leapfrogged grades and in two years had reached Grade 5. He was obviously a bright lad and was already chattering away in passable if amusing English. Occasionally the freedom of the street called and he disappeared for a few days, and once he committed some quite heinous crime but so ineptly I forgave him, managed to keep him out of prison and he always returned. When the Eritrean air force bombed Aider elementary school in Mekelle, killing and maiming many innocent children, Tammy then maybe 15 adjusted his age and enrolled in the military. For well over a year nobody heard anything of him as tens of thousands of soldiers were reported dead in a trench border battle at Badme that seemed reminiscent of the 1st World War. Daily I anxiously scanned the international press and war photographs until one day he reappeared in Mekelle seeking medical treatment for shrapnel in his leg. Despite his apparent bravery and offered promotion he begged not to return to fight. Now a "National Patriot & Hero" we arranged that he should return to school. I had to return to the UK and was having a last cup of tea and the ubiquitous bombalino with Tammy when I saw quiet tears running down his face. Ethiopians don't cry or sob like Westerners, so I decided to take Tammy for an evening walk and Tammy chose to go to a nearby reservoir where, as a trainee Commando, he had been taught to swim. Again an odd pair, I, awaiting a heart operation, was breathless and Tammy was limping due to his shrapnel wound. I tried to give advice about managing his scholarship allowance so as to be better able to eat regularly. Tammy said he once didn't eat for five days and when pressed said that was because of the smell when he was burying all his friends, none of whom had survived this war. I was too overwhelmed to ask anything more although it came out in pieces over the years. Young Tammy's story is long, too *long to tell here. He went on to get a Diploma as an Auto Technician and a truck driving licence and is generally in work. To "help" an abandoned boy is never easy and often requires more time, care and love than anyone else - but with Tammy, I know that he has made a worthwhile life for himself and his new wife and son and I am inordinately proud of him.*

The term "street boy" is derogatory and not really an acceptable term. That these abandoned, maltreated youngsters, often runaways, know full well that life is not fair does not detract from their resourcefulness and independence. I have met and hold a deep respect for some of these incredible youngsters; there is little they can be taught about self-sufficiency. They are the experts on survival and it has often made them, with good reason, very suspicious of anyone who wants to "help" them which often means exploitation. Sure they are very smart and can be ultra devious; in a way it is almost a sort of perverse pleasure to be manipulated by these slick operators. Within limits I can accept being "taken advantage of", why not? After all, during their lives they have been denied love, care or formal education and have generally had a rotten deal. Why should they not try to even things out a bit? They have their dignity and pride and, understandably, can be very sensitive. Unfortunately A-CET has not always been successful with these and other abandoned youngsters, the term of dismissal is "too much street in them" which I find hard to accept. I wish I knew the answer, in a way I admire their freedom and I see them as a great resource of un-channelled talent. To categorize youngsters into successes or failures would be far too simplistic and I can't accept these terms. No one is a failure; some just do better than others. Ethiopians have a rapacious appetite for learning and seem quite unfazed by examinations. None consider education an entitlement or right; to them it a precious and much valued privilege. Essentially Ethiopians seem programmed for success and they do have problems coping with rejection or perceived failure. Deeply fatalistic and religious, failure is sometimes thought of as a punishment or higher judgement. Although none of our students have ended their lives due to examination failure, it does happen, sadly too often. Their endurance for suffering and hardships seems to know no bounds. Their faith and fortitude seems to sustain them. Some of our students have severe problems coping as their parents and elder siblings die of AIDS; they are in need of especial support. To date A-CET has lost no students to AIDS, although we must be realistic and prepared. Without exception all my Red Cross staff and drivers, some so very talented, with whom I worked in the Afar Region during the early nineties have since died of AIDS. What a lamentable loss of resources.

Since the relative peace of 1992 and with improved health care, there has been a population explosion in Ethiopia, now well over 80 or 90 million, (although reputedly there is more livestock). Well over half of this population are youngsters of school age. In the 1950s Emperor Haile Selassie was asked by a diplomat what was the population of his country. After some thinking he replied *"about 500"*, referring only to his royal household, the rest of the then 20 million population obviously did not figure in his calculations.

Generally in Africa orphaned children are looked after by an extended family. Following extensive protracted civil wars and AIDS there has been an explosion of orphans, more so than any family can cope. In an ideal world there should not be orphanages. In Africa, orphanages are generally not good places, all are overcrowded, some are horrendous and notoriously some are exploitative. Exceptionally some are so luxurious that those orphans admitted then become so alienated from their cultural environment that the youngsters find it difficult to reintegrate back into their communities and, more importantly, employment. In Ethiopia orphanage inmates are expected to be eternally grateful and humble - positively Dickensian. Few get much love or guidance and their institutionalized treatment can be corrosive and quite destructive. Food is minimal, water and toilet facilities are inadequate, discipline is often brutal and arbitrary, and love, kindness or care virtually non-existent. Most orphanage youngsters I have met just want someone to talk to and listen to them. Yet incredibly most of these children have an inner resilience and develop good social and survival skills. Whilst living off their wits some can be smart if tricky – yet they are often endearingly lovable, even if rogues. Above all they are fiercely independent and in their view, not in need of help, however well-meaning. I believe that it is important to respect them and their dignity as people.

Supporting youngsters through their education is nothing new, many expatriates support Africans, or youngsters from developing countries, with their schooling. Whilst most promise to continue this support after their contracts end unfortunately, as they take up the demands of their lives elsewhere, in practice very few do. Any worthwhile education takes 10 to 15 years and children "dropped" can feel a great sense of further abandonment and often think that they must have done something wrong. This happens when overseas sponsors write their students letters and, due to life pressures, suddenly stop writing. This leaves an unexplainable void in the student's life. These events have the potential to seriously undermine their growing self-confidence. To give a child the taste of education and then take it away seems unnecessarily and thoughtlessly cruel. I was determined that none of those eight youngsters I was helping would be left without the wherewithal to complete their education to the maximum of their ability. But this cost money, money which I did not have, so I turned to my family and friends in the UK for support.

After previously operating informally for a number of years, A-CET was born. At the end of 1997 it was formally registered as a UK charity "to support the education of vulnerable young Africans". We were then supporting no more than ten youngsters with modest monthly scholarships to allow them to continue with their education. This was being paid for from a few of my family and friends. On being asked, I can only smile and say *"No I had no vision, no dream, no message, no magic moment, nor any great revelation"* - it just seemed like a very logical obvious and straightforward thing to do, something that needed to be done. Many years later virtually all those initial youngsters are grown-up young men and the majority are still in regular contact with me, if not in some cases working indirectly or as volunteers for A-CET. Undoubtedly all are making a valuable contribution to their families and their country's future. All would agree that their lives have changed for the better and have more choices; successes by any standards.

A-CET's funding seemed to grow as my family and their friends told their families and friends, and as more donors came forward and more students were added, in an admittedly rather ad hoc manner. There was no shortage of earnest, often desperate candidates - all with heart breaking stories. All Africans and perhaps Ethiopians more so, yearn to learn as they rightly see it as their way out of cyclical pervasive poverty. Many millennia ago the Ethiopian Princess Makeda, better known to the world as the Queen of Sheba, sought out King Solomon, then reputedly the wisest man on earth. Princess Makeda went in search of knowledge which she deemed more valuable than all the gold, silver, ivory and gems on earth [see quote at the end of this book]. Maybe this desire for knowledge is built in to the genes of all Ethiopians. It was the union of King Solomon and the Queen of Sheba that produced the first Ethiopian ruler, Emperor Menelik I, so starting their great Solomonic dynasty that ruled Ethiopia until 1974. Emperor Haile Selassie's final words, arguably some of the most dignified recorded, as he was suffocated to death by dictator Mengistu: *"If it is the will of people, so be it"*. That was the end of their near three thousand year Solomonic dynasty.

A-CET's student selection is now more formalized and, of necessity and in line with our distinctly limited capacity, more restrictive. Bisrat selects our students through recommendations from the Bureau of Education, Bureau of Youth, Sports and Social Affairs plus the local Physiotherapy Centre for disabled candidates. Requests and recommendations to sponsor specific children from returning tourists may be well meaning but, to be kind, inappropriate and no longer accepted. No foreigner can be expected to assess and know the real truth behind an appealing youngster. With thousands, perhaps millions of vulnerable deserving youngsters desperately wanting educational support they know exactly the right story to tell to tug heart strings, which may have little basis in reality. My heart, famously bigger than my head, or A-CET's budget, admits to previously making a number of selection errors and I now try to distance myself as much as possible from student selection. This is not always a popular stance for either me or local Manager Bisrat, who has to live amongst the too many disappointed applicants. In Africa the expression "to sell your grandmother" to get an education can be no fanciful saying! Unlike a number of other charities who offer only short-term scholarships for a few years, A-CET maintains its policy of long-term support. This can mean an obligation of over 15 years financial commitment which, often with private college fees for their final three years, can be over £ 3,000. This is more than we originally launched A-CET with!

Whilst there are no school fees at Ethiopian government run schools, technical and vocational training centres (TVETs) or universities, there are a number of hidden costs for any student or their family in attending full-time education. There are a number of high fee paying private schools accessible only to rich families' children; yet built with private donations to international charities ostensibly targeting the poor and vulnerable. Yet these are being run as highly profitable businesses and is another story that upsets me deeply. How many donors know how their money is really being spent? But even to go to any "free" school needs basic clothes and footwear plus books and pencils. Students also need something to eat and somewhere to sleep and higher education is often only available in the cities. Loss of income by the children and their families whilst they are at school must also be borne in mind, and this is probably their biggest barrier to youngsters continuing their education. Following 18 years of bitter civil war, forced internal transportation and certainly two widespread famines with over a million deaths, families had been destroyed and broken up. Ethiopia must have a million or more orphans or abandoned children whose families could not afford to keep and feed them. The Tigray Region, centre of the Tigrean People's Liberation Front (TPLF), was the most affected and devastated of all regions in Ethiopia and this was further aggravated when an old border dispute with former allies newly independent Eritrea developed into a full-scale war around 1999. Eritreans and Tigreans had always been well integrated: they speak the same language and intrinsically have the same culture with many intermarriages. The border war saw all Eritrean men deported north to Eritrea and all those born of Ethiopian mothers in Eritrea deported south to Ethiopia, which in many cases they were visiting for the first time. Families were split up and thousands of youngsters came into Tigray, often alone and with no support. They arrived into communities and an environment still struggling to overcome decades of famines exacerbated by civil war and were not always welcome. This put an increasing strain on these communities which often had a barely extant social support network. About this time the effects of many deaths from HIV/AIDS were also being felt - another source of abandoned youngsters with no visible means of support. Civil unrest always hurts the most vulnerable and generally voiceless. First, the women and children suffer, then the sick and elderly.

The Ethiopian highlands are predominately and strongly Orthodox Christian. This faith is an integral part of their daily life and I feel that primarily it is this unshakeable faith that has kept them and their country together through their interminable struggles during the civil war, famines and starvation. Nurse Birhan's father (Mr Woldu) told me that after year on year of famine and losing his wife and daughters, he felt they must have all done such a terrible thing that God was punishing them. But like all Ethiopians, as ever the optimists, he said that as he and Birhan were saved, God must have something special for them to do. To see and listen to Mr Woldu is indeed to look on somebody who certainly seems to have been touched by God.

At first A-CET was administered in Ethiopia by my local Red Cross colleagues, but as it grew it became obvious that administering such an ever growing demand, as more students were added, was beyond their capacity. After some initial difficulties, and with some support and guidance from Mr Zemichael, an influential dedicated politician, ex-TPLF commander and much more, Bisrat Mesfin was able to register a new local NGO, now the charity "Ethiopian Youth Education Support" (EYES) and is its Manager. Bisrat is also an A-CET Trustee. EYES is the charitable organization that, with a very few dedicated, committed and trained staff, effectively does all A-CET's work in Ethiopia.

All EYES five operational and executive permanent staff are Ethiopians and ex-students, so know where they have come from; this helps them to identify and empathize with all our students and the ethos of our rural school building programme. EYES liaises with the government, selects schools to upgrade and build, lets tenders, contracts and supervises all construction. It selects, manages and cares for all the students. From the outset, Bisrat has been the undeniable lynch-pin at the helm of EYES and is now its Chairman and Chief Executive, bringing everything from his own background and experience. Without reservation I can say that I have never worked with such an able, competent and committed administrator in any country in the world. I could never find sufficient words of praise and indeed feel more than doubly blessed. My trust in him is absolute.

Bisrat remembers going to school when to sit on a chair they had to take their own. He remembers classes being abandoned or cancelled when teachers were arrested or during bombing raids. During the civil war, Mekelle city, situated in a hollow, was blanketed with the smoke of fires after over five days of relentless bombing. He remembers passing the spot where his school friend was shot dead by a stray bullet on their way to school. Above all he remembers the gnawing hunger and empty stomach which they filled with raw grain, garnered from passing food relief trucks, and water. The water made the dry grain swell and gave the illusion of being "full". He remembers passing his siblings as they changed school shifts and joking about large simmering pots of traditional "kai-wat" (literally red stew, full of peppery meat) awaiting their return home, to find no fire and empty pots. These memories can not easily, if ever, be erased.

In 1998 Bisrat graduated with his Diploma in Business Management at Mekelle Business College and by correspondence has a Diploma in Tourism with Distinction. That he has personally forgone further studies to ably manage EYES growth and success is a source of concern to me. His first paid job was as a print shop sales representative before he went on to set up and manage a new tourism agency in Mekelle for an Addis Abeba-based family firm. Initially EYES was run by Bisrat in addition to his paid tourism activities. At first we set up EYES in a temporary office with a desk, a chair and a cupboard in the corner of a small internet café. We paid no rent and could afford little else. In the UK I worked from a corner of my living room with my old laptop.

Bisrat, like most Ethiopians, is intensely and justifiably proud of his country and it was and is his great desire to promote all its incredible history and culture to all visitors. It is Bisrat's sincere and genuine love of his country that enraptures all overseas visitors as his "tourists" are generally high level documentary film makers, naturalists and research archaeologists. Undoubtedly he ran the best and most successful tourist agency in Tigray but his bosses were neither easy nor appreciative of his success and he left. Their loss was A-CET's gain. Through Bisrat's contacts his influential visitors came to know of A-CET. Bisrat's hosting of Senior TV correspondent Brian Stewart from the Canadian Broadcasting Corporation was the start. Brian's long-term support of Nurse Birhan Woldu and her family was the seminal moment when A-CET began to become more internationally well known. It was Brian's footage of the "dying" Birhan in a Mekelle clinic that was screened during Bob Geldof's initial 1985 Band Aid concert that mobilized the world's generosity to help Ethiopia. The legend of Birhan was born.

Internationally known "miracle survivor" of the 1984 famine is Nurse Birhan. Mr Woldu, her father had remarried and in 2003 the support and administration of Birhan and her six step siblings became A-CET's official responsibility, having previously being handled privately by Bisrat on behalf of CBCs Brian Stewart. Other overseas visitors hosted by Bisrat followed, notably BBC's Michael Buerk who, in 2005, came to film his "20 years on" revisiting the scenes and personalities who had been filmed during the height of the 1985 famine. It was Michael Buerk's initial reporting in 1984/5 when he interviewed Red Cross Nurse Claire Bertschinger which was viewed by pop musician Bob Geldof of the Boomtown Rats and mobilized him to "do something". He set up Band Aid, later Live Aid and the rest, as they say, is history. With Michael Buerk in 2005 came a reluctant ex-Red Cross Nurse (now Dame and Doctor) Claire Bertschinger to revisit the feeding centre where she had had to choose which of the thousands of dying malnourished and starving children were to get supplementary feeding from her inadequate supplies. During their 2005 filming Claire met up with a young man Girmay Assefa, whom she had known as an abandoned seven year old boy whose mother, unknown to him, had just died. In the refugee camp Girmay had attached himself to the "clean smelling all in white" Nurse Claire and they had became inseparable until Claire left. When Claire was reunited with Girmay in 2005 she learnt that due to lack of funds he had abandoned his education. Claire wanted to help, so A-CET acquired yet another student. Girmay Assefa has since graduated as a software engineer and now, with his wife and two young sons (Michael and David), they run their small yet successful computer business.

Claire returned to the UK after her cathartic experience with the BBC to write her life story "Moving Mountains" - generously donating half the royalties to A-CET. A film company Green Lions, known to Claire, made a superb complimentary 15 minute documentary about A-CET "Learning for Life", all about our work which helped "to tell the A-CET story" to a wider audience. After this publicity famine survivor Birhan interviewed on Michael Buerk's film became a renewed source of now international interest and, (now Sir) Bob Geldof, was persuaded to re-release his money-spinning Band Aid song "Do they know it's Christmas". With financial support from the Sun newspaper they brought Birhan to London to *"tell this new generation of pop stars her, and Ethiopia's, famine story"*. We are fortunate that Dame Claire has recently joined A-CET's governing board in a very active capacity, bringing with her, a life-time's experience and a determined 'can do' philosophy, tempered with a real concern.

During the Derg regime Bisrat and his father had been forcibly transported north to Eritrea, whilst his mother and other family members were sent to relief camps in the south. A number of Bisrat's elder brothers became lost; his family, like so many, did not have an easy time. At that time the Derg government only controlled the main towns in Tigray, so they controlled all the relief food supplies which were only distributed in these towns. Food distributions were used as a means of rounding up all the population with an armed military forcibly putting them on trucks or planes to relocate them out of Tigray. This was a deliberate policy of depopulating the region in an attempt to prevent, particularly the rural population, from covertly supporting the TPLF fighters. The policy failed, but it caused massive dislocation of all families and exacerbated existing hardships.

Bisrat's father is a highly educated, well read and articulate person who worked for the government. Like so many educated people at that time, during the Derg he came under suspicion. Like so many fathers before and after, mistreatment and often torture destroyed them and their minds and they reacted in a variety of ways. Some took solace in alcohol or violent behaviour and some vegetated away blankly. Now Bisrat's father is an active scrivener and petition writer sitting on stones under a tree and a plastic awning outside the municipal offices where he helps the illiterate write their appeals. He calls Bisrat his "English son".

> *Desta Afewerki's story. Desta came to A-CET through the Red Cross as a high achieving Grade 10 student, but one who was constantly absent from school. On completing his Grade 4 his farmer father stated that he had enough education and it was now time for him to start helping full time on the farm. Desta was desperate to learn more, so at barely 11 he walked for over two days to Mekelle and enrolled at school where he continued to excel at his studies. But he knew nobody and needed to eat so, being a big lad; he took labouring jobs and slept under a street kiosk. After enrolling with A-CET he did well from the outset and soon graduated with a degree in accountancy. Importantly he has made peace with his father and is now a self-employed businessman. Desta helps Bisrat as a committed Director of EYES.*

> *Desta BA Accounting, self-employed, wrote: "When A-CET found me I was in a financial crisis with no food, clothes, shelter and my education discontinuing. I met David and joined A-CET. He shares his life experiences and grateful advice to*

study. I never forget that day ... really A-CET gave me a proper ladder for my future. Without its encouragement my hopes would not come to reality or fruition ... I now have a bright future and full confidence to develop good social conduct. I've visited many students and I see how they feel loved and have improved their life's condition through A-CET. Building elementary schools in remote areas to encourage poor farmers to educate their children is another issue which renders special appreciation for this organization. I am proud to be an A-CET member".

Until their London visit in 2005 Birhan had never left her home town: she knew nothing of hotels, air flights, escalators or lifts - and at that time had little English. She was the daughter of a struggling subsistence farmer, young, incredibly beautiful and possessed of a serene quiet dignity. Her world was her family home, her church and, recently, her government-run agricultural college. To take her to the capital city to get a passport and UK visa; to arrange a female companion/chaperone, both with suitable wardrobes, was a challenging administrative, bureaucratic and time-consuming task. Throughout, Birhan was accompanied by the ever resourceful, ever patient, EYES Manager Bisrat. A sceptical British Consular Officer initially refused their visas demanding proof of income, even marriage (none were married), bank books and proof of return etc etc. At that time the newly built British Consular Office had the aura of a hushed library or church. Certainly no one had ever dared question these custodians of UK visas to that promised land of perceived riches in England. On remonstrating at the impracticality of these demands within the time-frame, I was unceremoniously escorted off the Embassy premises by their security guards before a disbelieving and astounded audience of hopeful Ethiopian and Somali visa applicants. *"How dare I question their authority"* the diminutive Consular officer trilled. Suffice to say that after a UK phone call, routed through the UK Prime Minister's Office (Birhan and Bisrat had met Tony Blair with Sir Bob Geldof in December 2004 whilst they were attending the Commission for Africa conference in Addis Abeba), visas were granted that afternoon by the British Ambassador. It should not have to be like this, and visas continue to be increasingly difficult to obtain for our students and visitors. Personal contact with the UK Consular Officer is now made virtually impossible as all visa applications are handled through a private agency. Multi-page applications are only accepted on-line, not the easiest thing to do in Ethiopia, even in the capital where there is limited broadband access. The Consular Officer told me: *"We don't speak to applicants or their sponsors".* Why so difficult, in Indonesia and Kenya I had had such good relations with our Embassies and High Commissions. I was reminded of Sir Winston Churchill who once said: *"Our civil servants are neither civil, nor give a service".*

Subsequent missed flight connections and lost bags contributed to Birhan and party's excitement. But this was to be as nothing compared to their next invitation to appear on the Oprah Winfrey Show in Chicago, USA for her "Children who changed the world" series. I was ever mindful of the need for Birhan to return to college in time to continue her studies, and tried to decline this invitation. CBC's Brian Stewart, Birhan's long time sponsor, intervened with *"no one ever refuses an interview to appear on Oprah Winfrey's show"* - North America's (or the world's) queen of talk show hosts. Birhan was then in London for Bob Geldof's re-recording session and I thought that it would be no problem to get a US visa from their Grosvenor Square Embassy. This was not allowed, they must return to the Addis Abeba embassy to get their visas. By now I was back in Mekelle with not the same quality communication links as from the capital. I fielded many post-midnight phone calls from the Oprah Winfrey show organizers, one finally requesting me to send their HIV negative certificates: *"Sure,"* I agreed, *"I'll do it tomorrow"*. *"No we must have them now."* So I set up a satellite dish and plugged in all the connection wires and managed to tap out the necessary e-mail and attachments. I am not the most confident or technically competent computer operator. Mostly self-taught but a quick learner and I have generally learnt much from my much calmer Ethiopian students. I can usually manage if it's intuitive and can cope with most problems if I'm not too tired. Power supply and connection speeds in Ethiopia can be erratic, but are fast improving. Perhaps the best advice I get to cope with a seemingly intractable frustrating problem is to switch off, have a coffee and try again. This time I managed.

"Rules" dictated that they had to fly back from the UK to get their US visas from the US Embassy in Ethiopia. Birhan, ever accompanied by Bisrat and her chaperone, had a passenger death in flight necessitating their return to Rome. Hours were lost so their eventual arrival in Ethiopia was much delayed. They arrived in Addis Abeba long after the US embassy had closed, yet they were scheduled to check in for their early flight to US via London again at 4 am the next morning. The US embassy was re-opened especially for them and the Consular Officer was so cooperative, positively magnificent. Some Ethiopians can wait unsuccessfully for over ten years for a US visa; Birhan's party received all their US visas within ten minutes. The power of Oprah reaches far, as obviously Oprah gets what Oprah wants.

Birhan's appearance on the Oprah show was accompanied by Bisrat as translator. CBC's Brian Stewart had flown down especially from Toronto. The show was the usual emotional tear jerker that is Oprah's speciality. Apparently Birhan moved the audience to one of the few standing ovations ever on the show. Four months later and after much angst the Oprah show finally refunded A-CET's expenses - but sadly A-CET received not a single donation. With much difficulty and personal pleading we managed to get Birhan readmitted later to continue her agricultural studies. Both the Ethiopian embassies in the US and Canada claimed that Birhan's appearance on the Oprah show was the best publicity Ethiopia had had for over twenty years. So perhaps some good(will) had come of it. Although the stress and many sleepless or disturbed nights of making all these arrangements had made me feel distinctly older, I had learnt much in handling the fickle selfishness of some very demanding media.

Following Birhan's appearance on the world's stage I was plagued with international media requests. We had a plummy voiced journalist from one of the more right wing anti-immigration UK Sunday newspapers who entered the country as a tourist, circumventing the strict Ministry of Information's bureaucratic constraints. In those days, before a mobile network was established, she freely used our satellite phone without recompense. Surprisingly for the paper she wrote for, she was their only black reporter and at our final dinner together she asked Bisrat if he was surprised at her colour. *"Oh"*, Bisrat replied, *"I hadn't noticed"*. This reporter published her factually questionable article without any promised link, referral or acknowledgement to A-CET. I hope I'm a little wiser now and wasn't sorry that she failed to get any interview or quote when the story got much bigger after London's Hyde Park Live Eight concert. Her question about her colour reminded me of an earlier encounter with a doubtless well meaning acquaintance at a dinner with my adopted son Brima and others in an upmarket Golf Club in the UK. After nervously parrying the subject for a while he finally asked Brima what is was like to be black in the UK. Brima looked at his hands and feigning shock turned on me accusingly and said *"David I'm black, I'm black, and you never told me"*. End of conversation; we still have such a long way to go, but at least we have moved on from when people actually spat at Brima on a escalator in London's underground with some accompanying *"go home"* comment.

It is a constant quandary for me whether to give a media interview so as to ensure some semblance of truth or refuse and risk inaccurate sometimes mischievous reporting. These demands and misreporting by much media are a constant ever present dilemma for me and doubtless will be more so for Birhan throughout her life. Not unsurprisingly Birhan has developed a real aversion to insensitive probing media, especially about parts of her life that she would obviously prefer to forget. A number of quite misinformed reports about Birhan continue to be written and published for a "good story" with little semblance of truth. That we need the media I totally accept, but does it have to be always on their terms? Notwithstanding what I have written above, it would be remiss of me not to record how sensitive and supportive have been Chief Features Editor Oliver Harvey and veteran Photographer (by Royal Appointment) Arthur Edwards from the much maligned UK Sun Newspaper. The highest accolade that can be bestowed on you in Ethiopia is to say you are family. They are truly accepted as family. The exception that proves the rule, and I don't forget those Toronto Star guys I met in Somalia.

My initial intention with A-CET had only been to complete the education of my first small group of students. I later accepted there would be more students, but tried to limit these to about a hundred. I felt I could remember a hundred names, their backgrounds and grades and give them that personal attention they all needed and craved. With the explosion of international interest following Birhan's appearance on the world stage and my reluctance to say no, this rose once to well over 500. 300 more were accepted from another local Mekelle-based AIDS support agency. Selection of students became more formalized and Bisrat worked with the then Office of Rehabilitation and Social Affairs together with the local Physiotherapy Centre to identify those most vulnerable students who would not be able to continue attending full-time education without our support. The Physiotherapy Centre was managed by Mr Girmay, a local ex-Red Cross employee with whom I had previously worked. The Centre's operation is overseen by a committee comprising the Veterans Association, Red Cross and the Bureau of Health, and is the only Orthopaedic and Physiotherapy referral centre in the region. To be disabled in Africa, or indeed many parts of the developing world, is to be stigmatized and, traditionally, by the uneducated, often regarded as cursed - a punishment by God – and so fit only for a life of poverty and begging. Disability was not only the congenital club foot, recent land mine and war injuries, but thousands of youngsters, deprived of polio vaccinations during the civil war, were suffering from polio. A number had also suffered permanent paralysis through inexpertly given injections. I realize we will not change public perceptions overnight but after ten years I am proud of our first disabled undergraduate graduated in 2010 as a Water Engineer and has been selected for a Masters post graduate degree course. Other undergraduates are scoring the highest grades in the challenging disciplines of law and civil engineering. *"Slowly people are realizing that a disabled body does not mean a disabled mind"* says law student Yohannes Arkebe from his "flying" (winner of national competitions, he goes very fast) speedy wheel chair, locally made from bicycle parts. Now this is some sort of progress indeed.

Yohannes A's story. As a child Yohannes was either dropped or fell, with the outcome that his legs never worked again. With no mother or father, his aunts, struggling like so many to make ends meet, decided he was not worth feeding any more as he "was of no worth". His grandfather took him away into the country and fed him, but eventually died. Yohannes then crawled to the main road to get the bus back into Mekelle city as he yearned to go to school and learn. He had no money but the bus passengers joined together to pay his fare. Yohannes started cleaning shoes. He couldn't walk or stand up so, he says, as he was already at shoe level it seemed a good place to start. Noticed by the Physiotherapy Centre Manager, Mr Girmay, and found to be beyond any treatment or physiotherapy, a wheel chair was made for him out of scrap bicycle parts and Yohannes became mobile. Bright at school he was recommended to Bisrat and accepted as an A-CET student. Yohannes is articulate; he considers his disability is only as perceived by others when some able bodied people are often lazy and achieve less than he does. He is now an undergraduate in Mekelle University's law faculty - but there are few disabled facilities, no lifts or ramps. It can not be easy for him, tenacious and determined as he is. When Yohannes was accepted at University his aunts invited him back into their home, unashamedly saying that they could see that he was "worth something now". Family is very important to all Ethiopians, yet Yohannes declined. He said he has a new family now - A-CET.

Yohannes writes (sic):

"When I came to A-CET I had several problems. We humans need three things: food, clothes and shelter - but I can't find them because I am a disabled boy. I am a student but can't continue my education. A-CET solved all these problems. Thanks to God to introduce me to A-CET to change my life by education. Now I'm very happy in my life learning without any problems. Thanks to A-CET like my family. They are like mother and father giving advice, life experiences and morals with love. To Ethiopian young students and our country's problems A-CET understands. To solve these problems we need education. Now I'm in University and I have a big dream to change my life and my country by education. I hope I will be successful in my dream because my A-CET family are with me at any time. I'm proud of them and I will be strong and study hard. Education is key in human life and can break the big problem of poverty that we have. We the A-CET family students are the bright future men of tomorrow"

I was never totally happy with the idea of A-CET just supporting sponsored scholarship students. Sponsoring individual students by individual donors, whilst internationally popular by many agencies and providing a regular donation stream, has some often little appreciated negative sides. Larger agencies employ many field workers to constantly oversee and supervise these sponsored students. These field staff arrange student's letter writing and constant photo opportunities. We do not and can not afford to do that, even if I thought that was the best use of donated money, which I do not. For a small, still un-staffed, charity it can be extremely time consuming. Administratively student and donor's records need to be carefully maintained. All our students need individual care, counselling and guidance. Often our new, well meaning, dedicated donors, many with little real understanding or appreciation of the conditions our students live in, need to be appraised and kept informed of their student's progress. Additionally sponsoring individual students can support only that limited number and it is a considerable commitment over a long period. I hope I am not misunderstood, student sponsorship is great and has produced some outstanding results amongst our youngsters whose lives have undoubtedly been changed in a very positive way, but our size limits how many we can properly look after. We now have nearly 300 scholarship students and as our student's graduate, we are trying to reduce this to a more manageable figure, maybe I was right originally with a hundred after all!

Increasingly the charity world is a demanding cut throat business and A-CET has been unable to solicit larger donations from any big givers as we had no track record - individual sponsors were, and continue to be our regular life blood. I have previous experience of submitting professional grant proposals but Comic Relief, Lottery Fund, Princess Diana Fund and many more, turned us down - more than once. A-CET was too small, had no track record and one even inferred that I was too old.

Mahider's story. Mahider was born with Duchene's muscular dystrophy. This is a terminal and crippling illness only contracted in boys who, if lucky, then have little over 20 years life expectancy. There is still no known cure or ameliorating treatment. This inherited gene is carried only by women who do not manifest the illness. Mahider was a normal lad until, at six, paralysis started affecting his legs and walking became difficult. Now classed as disabled and cursed, and at a time when most needing the maximum family care and support, his grandparents threw him and his single mother out of their home. This would disassociate their family from this curse, and avoid the perceived contamination/contagion. Mahider came to see me and had tried to walk, but it was a rocky climb and he was covered in scratches where he had continuously fallen. His six years with us before his inevitable early death were an absolute joy which he spread among every-one he met. He sang and even looked like an angel. Within months he was fluent and articulate in English and computing skills and popular with all he met.

After completing his Grade 9 promotion examinations Mahider wrote:

"Before A-CET I was a lazy student. I started schooling but I don't even know what the function of education was. Bisrat visits me when I was Grade 3 and I join at Grade 4. He told me about A-CET and gave advice. It's beyond my capacity to talk about A-CET but it has changed my and my family's life. I get scholarship and A-CET donors encourage me that I'll have a bright future. Now I understand that if you make the effort nothing is impossible. I try to make the effort and to work hard and I became hopeful and became top student every year. Before I was not able to even read, write or speak English and I go to language academy and within a short time I can manage fluently. A-CET is my life and I'd like to thank all its supporters of this work. I'm proud to say that A-CET is doing a good thing ... my family love A-CET so much".

Just before he knew he has passed, as usual, top in his Grade 9 exam, after a very brief illness Mahider sadly died, he was barely 17. If ever any of our children looked like a messenger from God, it was Mahider. His younger cousin, an elder sister's baby abandoned at birth, has developed the same symptoms at six years old. Simon, an A-CET student, increasingly disabled, is being lovingly looked after by Mahider's dedicated and ever patient mother. Her dedication and devotion to Simon is humbling.

I believe that A-CET is professionally run, we are transparent, open and honest and from 2001 have been winning recognition, commendations and awards from professional organizations for the best Annual Report and for our contribution to international development through education. Our donors are generally not rich people, with many are from the caring professions, nurses, teachers and carers. From the outset our donors have proved themselves to be dedicated and committed. A-CET spends what donations it receives and is unable to afford much advertising, let alone build up any reserves. My long-time friend and Auditor/Examiner Michael for years charged nothing for his work and advice, although now we have grown too big for him to manage as his work principally is overseas. He still constantly advises me, or would harangue be a better word, to build up some reserves, not easy. Our fund-raising is talking to schools and often in church halls, to women's and professional organizations, where and when invited. Sometimes I barely raise enough for my travelling expenses, yet I keep moivated by saying it is all increasing awareness and sowing seeds for the future.

I can understand wanting that "feel good" factor - we all crave it. Donors or volunteers deserve it and charities rely on them for so much of their continuing work. Volunteering is a more committed form of donating. Those without money may have time. More than most I should be able to appreciate the mind set of volunteering as I consider myself a volunteer and I appreciate that part of what I write now may be unpalatable to some. Many who volunteer are not always suitable and can be offended when rejected. The concept of "going to help the poor in Africa" is no longer enough; it should have never been enough. The best of the missionaries, leaving aside the treasure hunters, the selfish and the traders may have meant well, but overall sometimes they were responsible for terrible damage to peoples, their cultures and beliefs. And that is discounting the very bad missionaries.

Volunteers should ask themselves why they want to volunteer, to do what, what are your skills, what can you offer, can you fit in with their culture? Remember often that what we do here in our own culture may be quite alien where you want to go. Volunteering should not be like a package tour. Think about the real and hidden costs of those hosting you. What are the total costs of your volunteering and would not this money be better employed in the country you want to go to? Are you trying to escape or travel, do you want to enhance your CV? Try to be honest with yourself. I have accepted and looked after a number of volunteers and I have met others volunteering. With some very notable superb exceptions, many have not been easy and often wasteful of time, money and resources. My advice, if you really want to volunteer in Africa, is to get or come with a useful practical qualification, learn how to teach it and come and teach people to do your skill or profession. Volunteering in your own country, a charity shop or stuffing leaflets in envelopes for a mailing may be less dramatic, but is often worth far more to any good cause. Yet because I have met and used some fantastic inspirational volunteers who have that skill to immediately relate wherever they go, I will still use them, but after very careful selection. Unfortunately a common mistake by many English speakers is that they can just go overseas and teach English. This is not the case.

Posting "gifts" to developing countries is also not always appropriate, whether new or used. Out-of-date or unsafe medicines can be lethal. Clothing is often highly inappropriate. Pretty carefully wrapped little Christmas shoe boxes often contain items that deprive local traders of their business and dental floss is not required! Toys and dolls are a joke, who wants a doll when there are so many little children that can be cuddled and carried around. Footballs are much valued and prized, but can be better bought locally. Thank you but no thank you.

From my earliest days with A-CET and maybe before, I became vaguely aware of the power of the internet. From 1998 A-CET had a mini web-site but it had no secure donation link, this was after all relatively early days. In 2000 it all changed with the launch of our first web-site prepared by family friend James, a professional new media and web designer with his own business Publitek New Media.

The web-site brought an increasing number of enquiries and particularly one from a consortium of European International Schools through their newly formed "Global International Network" (GIN) set up by Clayton Lewis the visionary Director of the International School in Luxembourg. This helped A-CET change its direction to become more effective and help more youngsters with better access to quality education. As a part of their new International Baccalaureate syllabus included practical participation in an overseas development project and Maria Perreau contacted us, GIN wanted to partner with an organization on real educational development projects. This was the break through we were looking for at A-CET without probably realizing it ourselves at the time. GIN wished to fund the development of rural elementary schools. Through EYES and with the local Education Bureau we were directed to an area in most need of schools development, which coincidentally was in the very area where I had worked with the local Red Cross during the mid nineties and where I believe I am both well known and trusted. A-CET was offered a number of options and initially selected a struggling school called "Fikre Alem" (meaning World Love) in Aderak village. It had little more than 200 pupils studying in an assembly of leaky, dusty stone shacks with little furniture. But the teachers were dedicated and the community was keen. Initially funds were strictly limited and A-CET was only able to help put in concrete floors and supply local-made basic furniture. Previously the students sat on stones. It was a start but within a year we had galvanized more supporters and raised sufficient funds to support the local community to complete four blocks of sixteen basically furnished, bright, airy, and cool, locally quarried and dressed stone classrooms, now accommodating over eight hundred students from Grades 1 to 8 (years 1 to 8).

Aderak village school became our flagship project on which we at A-CET were able to build our reputation, not only in the local community but also with our donors, old and new, without which we would not have been able to fund any more projects. Early on we made a number of mistakes but we learnt from them. Always our guiding principle was that the village must want a school and that they should have shown some commitment in already starting one, however basic. We learnt how to identify dodgy contractors, how to manage impassable roads during the rainy season, how to be assured of cement during national shortages, importantly how to involve and motivate the community, how to keep our donors on board and informed and, above all, how to work with the local administration and infrastructure. After all these were government run "free attendance to all comers schools" and the government provided the staffing and maintenance costs – so the schools we helped to build were self sustaining from day one.

By helping communities to upgrade and build these new village schools, A-CET was helping to bring closer access to better quality education to children previously denied any education unless they walked for hours, often through wild lands with marauding packs of baboons, scavenging hyenas and red foxes, to their nearest school. Families, often with illiterate and innumerate parents, were initially sceptical about the value of education and doubtful about losing their children's labour in tending their flocks or helping around their farms - but if the school was nearby, and they had helped to build it, they soon began to appreciate the value of an education and were more willing to release their children to go to school. School registrations soared.

By 2005, as A-CET was building its second school in an isolated off road village, we still had no vehicle and either relied on a loan from the Bureau of Education or often distinctly unreliable, expensively rented, four wheel drive Land Cruisers driven by owners or their friends with limited off-road experience. This was unsustainable and often unsafe. Occasionally I travelled on a mule; but they were slow, uncomfortable, stubborn and flea-ridden. After eight years, by much financial juggling, we managed to order our first vehicle and employ our first local civil site-engineer. Donors are generally happy to fund projects but with good reason often baulk at funding what they see as "overheads". How do we administer ourselves and get around? Our capacity and ability to monitor our school projects and out of town students better was transformed overnight. At about the same time, working out of the corner of an internet café was no longer proving practicable, and A-CET rented a modest four room bungalow near the centre of town as an office for our partner EYES. Under Bisrat's charismatic leadership EYES was fast becoming a strong and effective partner for A-CET. In the UK A-CET continues to be run from my small council flat, at the beginning alone but now supported by a band of dedicated professional volunteers and later some Ethiopian post graduate students studying in the UK. Sammy was the first.

> *Sammy's story. Just before we moved out of our internet café office there was disturbance at the local university. Several students were attempting to e-mail their families or relatives to either assure them of their safety or request funds to return home. History shows that in developing countries many coups are fermented within universities, and Ethiopia was no exception. The first attempt to overthrow Emperor Haile Selassie in 1974 was by the very students he had sent*

to the US for study - being dissatisfied at the apparent lack of reform on their return. This has encouraged African governments to be rather brutal when dealing with any student dissent, even seemingly mild complaints about inadequate food or unclean drinking water. Mekelle University was unsettled, some students were locked in, others locked out and classes were suspended. The police were nervous and some well spoken articulate students counselling calm were often mistakenly targeted as ring leaders. Sammy was one of these. The internet café where we still had our office only boasted two computers, and connections, when made, were invariably slow, so there was a queue and long wait. I took one of the waiting students to lunch, to the same lady who had in fact cooked my first meal in Mekelle with Bisrat so many years earlier. Sammy was obviously very hungry and ate well, very well, and our friendship developed. Graduating a few years later as an Industrial Engineer he became our first UK post graduate student and my indispensable assistant with A-CET's work in the UK. Now on a Wellcome Trust fellowship he is completing his PhD into malaria genome research at Cambridge's Sanger Research Institute. Yet only a decade ago he, with thousands of others, was sitting in a mud floored, brush wood walled, badly roofed grubby dark classroom. What more untapped potential could there be out there? It was Sammy who in 2007, addressing a hall full of High Court Judges in the Royal Courts of Justice in the Strand closed to a standing ovation with "Educate us and then we can develop Africa". Sammy, now an A-CET Trustee, regularly speaks internationally on awareness of A-CET's work - and also on malaria genome research for the Wellcome Trust. I feel truly blessed that Sammy has joined me in helping to run A-CET.

Sammy at 28, BSc Industrial Engineering, MSc Information Systems Management, and MPhil Computational Biology now a PhD researcher in Cambridge writes:

"Without A-CET's consistent care, support and encouragement, I doubt I could have got the distinctions that have helped me get where I am today."

By any international standards Sammy has done well, very well, and obviously is possessed of extraordinary potential. He has a highly developed social conscience and a maturity that belies his youth. But how well would he have done without A-CET support? Undoubtedly the potential was always there. When his Cambridge Research Director asks me if we have any more students like Sammy, I am lost for an answer. A-CET does not accept students on their academic ability but on their need for support to continue to attend full-time education. Nevertheless students who join us invariably become high achievers proving a latent potential. Students like Sammy are very rewarding and give a great sense of fulfilment, although it is they who have the dedication and do all the hard work. In so many ways they are self runners needing little encouragement. Those students who perhaps give me an even greater sense of achievement are those difficult "abandoned" youngsters, the border-line, unloved, undisciplined, wild and troublesome lads. To be able to give them an education and steer them away from the attractions of drugs, pilfering and the easy buck can be frustrating, time consuming and a path strewn with let downs and disappointments, but it gives me a warm feeling of having done something worthwhile. This is truly changing lives in a positive way and giving these youngsters more life choices.

Decades of working in Africa, with the disciplines of civil engineering, management and latterly in the "development" field has taught me much. I have survived personal physical attacks, ambushes, land mines, mortaring, gunfights, kidnap attempts, wrongful arrests, coups, political intrigues and grudges; more than any cat's nine lives. How? Basically by listening to whoever I was with and trusting them implicitly and taking few risks. Africans, I soon learnt, have an innate sense of survival - with that level of competence, ingenuity and intelligence that can, with a little support, prove them quite capable of helping themselves. I have seen so many expatriate "experts" who come and dictate hair brained, impractical, nationwide schemes that have wasted millions of pounds (actually usually dollars) and often caused much damage, let alone leaving a local population cynical and disillusioned. I quote from Abba Paulos, Patriarch of the Ethiopian Orthodox Church who referred to this on opening a school we built for abandoned, orphaned often disabled youngsters training for a life-time's service in the church:

"Many expatriates come and go with achieving nothing, but Teklebrhan (Mister David's baptised name) lives with the spirit of Ethiopians and Tigrean peoples' culture and tradition. He lives by sharing all the joy, the pain and the love of the people. He shares his skills, his money and his energy with the people. We feel he belongs to us and is a great man. God bless him! He is baptized in our Orthodox Church as Teklebrhan, [bringer or plant of light]. All in all he preaches to the people to learn more and more since this is the source of civilization. Education is an instrument for development; a weapon to eradicate poverty. Let other humanitarian people follow Mister David's example to share their money, their vision and their love to the vulnerable children like ours. God bless Ato Teklebrhan!"

I remembered the sunburnt pigs and lazy bees from Tuvalu. And do Africans really need an expensively printed book on how to mix concrete by hand? I have experienced inordinate waste, unchecked large-scale corruption and wanton, unjustifiable expenditure. I have witnessed fellow expatriates living pretentiously at standards far beyond their home styles and, embarrassingly, lording it over patient ever tolerant local staff. It had all sickened me and I was determined not to let A-CET follow these routes. I appreciate that most of our donors are of limited means and when they donate to A-CET I am determined to make their every penny, or cent, count.

I know Swahili and can still curse roundly in West African Krio, so why, I have been asked, was I working in Ethiopia where I am no linguist, often understood little and could not express myself well? Initially A-CET was supporting students in Tanzania and Kenya and we tried to build a school for 400 war orphans near Makeni, Sierra Leone. But when the Pastor ran off to the US with the second instalment to put the classroom roof on, I realized I was wasting more than my time and our donor's money. A-CET now only works in Ethiopia in an area where corruption is unacceptable and where all with whom we work are totally dedicated to do the job for their own and their country's pride. The Ethiopians with whom A-CET and I work are honest (with trust the vital ingredient), backed up by a technical and professional competence. Yet be sure that I do not see everything though rose-tinted spectacles. Ethiopians are superb diplomats, extremely discreet to the point of often revealing little. I can work with this and remember some advice given before I first left for Ethiopia with the Red Cross: *"remember that Ethiopians can always get you to do what they want all along, and by making you think it was your idea"*. Why not?.

To contribute any worthwhile lasting change in the educational sector in which A-CET only works after Education Bureau advice and direction, we first send our local representative, Bisrat Mesfin, to ask the local people what they want and we then help them to execute that. We work within local established power structures and the local government. We don't lobby or try to interfere in or criticize local politics or try to supplant existing structures, even if they may not quite "fit in" with our original ideas. Our only condition is that it is used as a school. What works in the UK, US or other parts of the world or even other African countries may not work where we are working now. I try to be tolerant and patient - things can often take an inordinate amount of time. I try to tell myself that anything good or worthwhile takes time. After all we waited patiently for over six months for the customs to release a donated vehicle. Time in Africa is measured differently.

I know I am not the most tolerant of people and I do not suffer fools gladly, so I often find this a challenge. I recognize that meetings are important and in Africa these may go on for hours, if they are not delayed by days or weeks. In village communities everyone will want to speak, even if what they say has been said before. As a ferengi (expatriate) I try not to go or show myself at any proposed new project until funding is almost assured. I never promise what I can't deliver. Any visit by an expatriate may create expectations and, despite Africans having seen too many of us fly in, promise the world and fly out having done nothing, people always live in hope and hear what they want to hear. Consultants and short-term contract personnel may pad their CVs with overseas visits, but to me they have little credibility. Any overseas organization that thinks it can come and direct a development project alone is not only mistaken, but to me displaying the height of arrogance. Just how would we feel if a group of overseas experts from a different culture came, say from Korea, and told us how to develop our own communities and education?

From its inception A-CET has only worked and continues to only work in the educational sector. Too many small NGOs and charities diversify into planting trees and seeds, irrigation, hill terracing, providing water, building roads and health centres. All well worthwhile and very necessary components and probably much needed projects. But if you are not an international charity with near limitless resources like Oxfam, Save the Children, Red Cross or World Vision, is this wise? Surely it is better to specialize and do what you do well, to the exclusion of all else?

How do I keep A-CET going? To operate in any way A-CET needs money. We have already seen that in the highly competitive cut throat, increasingly business-like charity world, big donors are few and far between. Within years of launching our web-site we have made two significant total re-designs and this has been a great source of revenue which we now get from over twenty countries world wide. Increasingly we have posted short high definition videos of our work on the web-site. All our donors are deeply valued and I try to tell them so and keep them "on board". To every donor I write a personal thank you note and through the web-site, newsletters and our annual magazine with accompanying DVDs, all are kept fully informed of where their donation is going and what a real difference it is making. After all this seems to me only common courtesy and it has built up a steady retention rate of committed and dedicated donors with very few drop outs. Why do donors donate? I believe that they genuinely want to help others less fortunate than themselves, and, yes, they deserve their "feel good" factor. They want and are surely entitled to know where their money goes and how it makes a difference. I believe few of our donors are emotional donors who respond to emergency appeals. I do not credit the concept of donor fatigue, maybe it should be called charity fatigue in our not communicating well with donors.

A-CET gives presentations when and where invited, and only request expenses to be covered. Personally I do not consider myself a good marketing person, but I can talk convincingly from my heart on what I believe in. In truth our senior Ethiopians can do it much better than me. They draw bigger audiences and collect far more money than I ever do. Surely that's how it should be! A-CET never inflates its requests and always tries to be open and honest with its donors. At A-CET we value our independence and have steadfastly refused to become involved with any government grants or loans, neither do we accept any corporate giving in return for commercial introductions, favours or directed projects. I value this hard won independence. Repeat funding for new projects remains a continual challenge. A-CET has managed to maintain its income level, even during international financial downturns, as our income sources are wide and varied. I firmly believe that donations made are for spending on its charitable work. This is what donors donate for, not for maintaining millions in reserves as many large charities do. Yet I am always advised to maintain some level of reserves in case of a fall-off of donations; this is not easy when there always seems far more demand than we can meet.

A number of donors have travelled to visit our students and projects, often coupled with a trip as a tourist to a still largely unknown and misunderstood Ethiopia. That some have come again and again, should say something. Their visits are deeply valued as they help to affirm what A-CET is doing. Senior students generally host their visits and this improves their social skills. One of our young overseas visitors once burst into tears as she saw our rather shabbily dressed youngsters rehearing for an forthcoming circus performance, *"they're so poor"* she said - not realizing that they were quite unaware of how they looked and how rich they felt in friendship, love and care. The redemptive power of love knows no bounds.

Since my earlier heart operation and some laser work on my eyesight, I have always felt joyously fit, telling myself I had no time to be sick. Like all men I have little patience with sickness. Told by my sister I was becoming hard of hearing and tending to shout, I went for an ear test. After an hour long test I was given a hearing aid for my left ear and was scheduled for an operation on my right ear. This had to be postponed as I was about to fly out to Ethiopia. Relating this story to a priest in Ethiopia I was taken to an elderly hermit, Woldegiorgis reputedly over 100, who was living on a mountain. He was bed ridden and appeared to be blind, although I was later told he only saw heavenly things. Many hours of praying, laying on of his soft hands and pouring holy oil in my ear, I was blessed, dismissed and told I no longer needed an operation. Returning to the UK hospital again, I was re-tested by some computer-linked audio device in fact tested twice. The consultant was puzzled and told me the first tests must have been wrong as there was nothing wrong with my hearing in either of my ears. I was discharged and have not used a hearing aid since. I do not need to look for an explanation, as I was told all I needed was faith. Religions intrigue me but at this stage of my life I am still not confident enough to know the answer, if there is one. Maybe I question too much. I was very late to become a confirmed Anglican yet lost much of my faith in Zambia. I was attracted to the non-hierarchical concept and peace testimony of the Society of Friends (Quakers) but the practicing reality of it drove me away. In the Ethiopian Orthodox Church the strength of their nationwide belief and faith is palatable and after much instruction eventually in a dark incense filled room at about four in the morning amidst much chanting I became baptised as *"Teklebrhan"*, roughly translated as bringer, or plant of light. The priests murmured on the impossibility of getting *"this big baby into the font"* and I was taken to a corner of the room to be stripped totally naked and have freezing water and holy oil poured all over me. Once again in Africa I was so grateful to have been circumcised at birth! Whilst my Ethiopian family screened me off, I doubt if any of the mother's with their docile gurgling babies awaiting baptism, could see me in the gloom. It is impossible, if not dangerous, to generalise, but Ethiopia is roughly half Muslim and half Christian, both existing peacefully side by side. But there are some aspects of their strictly orthodox teaching: women priests, attitude to AIDS, and some corrupt behaviour, which trouble me deeply. I have yet to reconcile myself to this before I can be totally at peace with, and can write more about, their doctrine. Meanwhile let it just be said: I have faith and do believe, implicitly.

As A-CET continues to upgrade and build more government run, community rural elementary schools, it plans to maintain a number of individual scholars, although probably fewer than the current three hundred. All our visitors are so appreciative of the manner and care by these future movers and shakers of Ethiopia. So we will always have an important place in A-CET for individually sponsored students. Without exception, all our students have experienced the most traumatic backgrounds, yet they seem to wear their sorrows and traumas lightly, traumas that would surely destroy many in our more "developed" environment. I am not good at delving into our students' backgrounds, but sometimes when alone they may share parts of their life stories and I know it is important to listen. I believe within their bluff exteriors, many are essentially quite fragile. Some are brought up by their grandparents, the result of a government soldier's rape during the Derg. One lad's 13 year old mother died soon after childbirth; he was brought up by his grandparents whom he always took to be his parents and, with our support, has successfully graduated and is now employed. Very few know their fathers and too many mothers have died early, so children, if not abandoned, are being brought up by sometimes unwilling, struggling, unloving, often rapacious, uncles or aunts. Some orphaned girls would be collected by an avaricious older woman posing as their aunt, moved to another town only to be sold into servitude or worse. Mothers would routinely sell their "surplus" children. A child has a market value, despite slavery being long outlawed by Emperor Haile Selassie since the 1920s as a prerequisite to Ethiopia's being admitted to the League of Nations. Barely educated young girls are still "sold" through agents by their families into a life of degrading domestic employment in the Middle East. But not knowing of their family's desperation how can we judge? Their plight might be understandable, but not to those expatriates who attract children, some even on scholarships with us, with wonderful offers of a life of overseas, riches as circus performers, or a better education. Starry-eyed they drop out of school only to be later abandoned for a variety of reasons that don't bear contemplation.

If any Ethiopian member of family is imprisoned or is admitted to hospital they will not be fed by the State; that remains the responsibility of the remaining family. Nothing can better underline the meaning and importance of family. If you have no family basically you have no life and no future. Following the independence of and split from Ethiopia by Eritrea, one 11 year old watched his Ethiopian born mother die on a trolley in an Eritrean hospital corridor, denied treatment as a "dirty Ethiopian". Seeing little future in Eritrea, with his even younger sister, they walked south, following the sun, for many days until they were eventually picked up exhausted, hungry and asleep by an Ethiopian military border patrol. They were placed in a less than pleasant orphanage which denied them a continuing full-time education. Previously a top student the boy understandably became embittered, rebelled and eventually was excluded, which in his case meant onto the street. Taken in by A-CET, together with his sister, they now have their own rented furnished room and, whilst he still has his wilder more difficult moments, I believe his life is slowly coming back together as he now attends college as a diploma student whilst gaining valuable work experience in a leading photo studio. But all this takes time, faith and inordinate patience.

One student on graduating set up his own carpentry businesses and, on appearing successful, an absent father reappeared only to take over everything from him. Tough and resourceful this young man moved on and set up another similar successful business. To many of our students A-CET has become their family and at first I resisted, feeling uncomfortable at being called Father or Daddy. Not a role I seem to have been able to fulfil well in real life. Eventually I accepted that this was maybe the role that I was expected to fulfil and have done my best.

One lad abandoned at two to fend for himself by his HIV positive, "street working" mother, despite years of our care, has not found any school or even orphanage capable of managing him, yet we cannot abandon him. We try to keep him clean, clothed, fed and out of trouble but to take the "street" out of street children is no easy quick fix task. Another rescued as the only surviving child from the totally devastated Hawzien village following an Ethiopian Derg government bombing raid, whilst brilliant and intelligent, finally flipped in the last stages of his university and has become a rather lost confused soul possessed by all manner of demons. With no access to any established counselling services and abandoned by the educational system, how can A-CET leave him, who else have they? They may have "dropped out" of the system but I don't want to judge them as failures.

On a more positive note I include a few unsolicited extracts from our students' letters to me:

Ezana, BSc Industrial Electrical Engineer, employed, writes:

"A-CET means an organization that really changes the life of many students as well as mine. I don't know where I'd be without A-CET and I can't find enough words to express my feelings about how my life has changed. We Ethiopians are good organizers, give us the resources, we know what we need, and we can educate ourselves to develop our country".

Yohannes, BSc Business Management, employed and EYES Band Leader wrote:

"With A-CET we've come a long way together. I had bad family problems but with the support of A-CET, my sisters and I are getting a good support for our education and we are learning equally with our friends [all sisters have now graduated and are employed]. What we get from A-CET is not only money for

books, uniform and other necessary materials but advice on how to be motivated to study and change our lives. I don't know how to thank A-CET, they may be small but they're big in heart. Everyone thinks and lives their own lives selfishly, but those in A-CET work and care for us, so I will become caring like A-CET".

Abel BSc, Computer Engineering undergraduate wrote:

"Before A-CET I had so many problems with my education, health and family. These problems were cancelling my aims and intelligence and I felt desperate and useless. The day I met David was a greater day than other days, he asked me politely about my life situation and then he shared his life experiences, gave me advice and encouragement. A-CET fills this role in overcoming poverty through education and I'm so happy to get this chance".

Klbrom, BSc Computer Science, employed, wrote:

"Words fail to express my happiness at being an A-CET student. You gave me undivided attention taking care of me, teaching me in many ways and making me to act like myself, helping me to widen up my mind. A-CET is key of my life as education is the key to everything".

Kokob, BSc Civil Engineering undergraduate writes:

"When I was very young I became ill and was taken to hospital. They gave me an injection but that was not correct because afterwards my right leg became paralysed. So from that time, despite visiting hospitals even in the capital, I've been disabled. Elementary school was not so comfortable as I don't fit in the chairs. But through the Physiotherapy Centre in Mekelle I got an A-CET scholarship and I did well at Senior and High School. Now I'm the top achieving undergraduate in Civil Engineering at Admass University in Nazret, which has excellent facilities for disabled students. A-CET brings me brightness to my dark life like a candle and came to me at the right time. In A-CET there is not only the financial scholarship but psychological support which makes them different. My future plan is to become a well-known civil engineer in Ethiopia where I can help build up my country. My disability will not stop me from achieving my aim, with the support of A-CET and my family".

Through the International School GIN and Coornhert Gymnasium (a state secondary school) in the Netherlands, A-CET arranges live awareness presentation and briefing sessions, often led by Manager Bisrat, or Trustees Sammy and Dame Claire. The level of commitment and understanding of all teenagers is heartening and promises well for the future.

No professional fund raisers are employed, basically because we can't afford them, but principally because we believe an appeal from our hearts is far more effective. A-CET employs no intrusive street "face to face" fund raisers neither do we do national direct mail shots. Our donors are not harried with constant appeals but updated at least annually. A-CET does not lobby or campaign because it does not believe that is a proper charitable activity for us, nor does it align itself with any politicians or political party. A-CET's media presence is modest; we place minimal advertising, mainly to attract future legacy donors, as advertising is prohibitively costly. I continue to work from my flat and we still have no paid staff in the UK, but for how long this will be sustainable without A-CET having to employ someone and rent a small office is an imponderable. When A-CET was set up in 1997 we had to register and annually report to two government organizations. Now this is seven, yet "red tape" is allegedly being reduced! But how can A-CET afford to pay any staff, or rent a small office without spending funds desperately needed for projects and students in the field? Whilst there are a number of our senior graduated students whom I believe could admirably and efficiently run the fund raising and legal compliance for A-CET in the UK, increasingly impenetrable and restrictive immigration laws make this well nigh impossible in the long-term. So do we need to be located in the UK? Vital communications, so essential to effective working and ancillary services are still not easy or sufficiently reliable in Ethiopia.

Following Nurse Birhan's appearance at the 2005 Live Eight concert in London's Hyde Park, Bisrat approached Sir Bob Geldof for possible support and was directed to his Band Aid Trust - ably managed by Joe Cannon. When I was with the Ethiopian Red Cross in the early nineties, Bob Geldof and I occasionally passed in airports. Well I saw him (Bob is very tall) but I doubted that he ever noticed me! He was my hero even then but awe-struck, I was far too shy and never spoke. To see Bob Geldof in the then chaotic mêlée of the single terminal in Addis Abeba airport, this tall, gangly, essentially rather scruffy guy in a battered straw hat was enough for me. Bob had an aura and great presence; above all I remember his calm patience in this mad scrum to get on any plane. Once on returning to Mekelle, I tried to tell my group of lads about Bob Geldof. No one knew him although there were still a number of battered trucks trundling around with "Band Aid Trust" stencilled on. I brought Bob Geldof cassettes and his book "Is that it?" to help educate and motivate my lads. To me anyone who could tell the then dictator Mengistu that he was a thief (taking the relief food supplies to feed his military) and a murderer (deliberately starving and forcibly transporting thousands of Tigreans to the far south) must be a brave man of absolute conviction. The TV cameraman who was present at this interview later related to me that Mengistu feigned not to understand English, and his interpreter was far too diplomatic, or terrified, to translate Bob's exact words. The same cameraman said he feared arrest and knowing Ethiopian prisons served no food, filled his anorak jacket pockets with crisps and nuts from the snacks provided in the President's office "just in case".

Increasingly A-CET's relationship with the Band Aid Trust has developed and with it their financial support of our school projects. This culminated in Sir Bob Geldof and his party opening our fourth rural community elementary school at Hagere Selam (meaning "place of peace") on 24 November 2009. A very proud day for A-CET as Sir Bob declared *"Some charities can do it and some can't. A-CET is one of those that can."*

A-CET's priority is first and foremost to the thousands of children we are helping with easier, closer access to better education. Locally selected for vulnerability, not necessarily academic prowess, these youngsters, often orphans, and the abandoned or disabled, can and are achieving more opportunities through long-term free and easier access to better quality education. They do the study and we don't necessarily push them towards academic brilliance. However, a group of visiting international Band Aid Trust supporters asked why so many of our students were achieving so well. I just don't know, I've read much on the subject and I still don't know. Certainly I believe much of it is due to the dedicated and fully committed focussed hard work of our students, but what drives them? If this is partly due to our motivation and inspiration then we must be doing something right. Are geniuses made or do they develop? Do people naturally rise to the top? How much is due to the opportunity and of being in the right place at the right time? Would our students have ultimately done so well or as well without A-CET, but maybe taken longer? And what do I say to those who say please send us more Ethiopians like Sammy or MBA student Ysakor? There may well be thousands of potential geniuses out there but it would be totally impracticable for us to advertise; in the rather haphazard way that Africa seems so well to operate, they seem to find us. A-CET is satisfied as long as our students continue to be committed to study to the best of their ability and they learn how to be kind, unselfish and pleasant people. I am aware that this can sound very corny in our developed world. Through our support we try to give our students financial security, pride in themselves and confidence, and above all we try to fit them for a world they already know is not fair with most of the odds stacked against them.

Shamelessly I admit that I still get emotional, very emotional. When our EYES Band played the 1984 Band Aid fund raiser song "Do they know it's Christmas" for Sir Bob Geldof and his Band Aid Trust supporters and friends, my eyes were blind with salt tears and I had to stumble away. I am still unable to watch Michael Buerk's seminal BBC documentary on the Ethiopian 1984 famine or any documentary of such abject suffering. I know every one of those suffering children in 1984 is dead except, miraculously, our Birhan Woldu. I start it to show this film to groups and creep out of the room. When I am no longer affected by these tragedies maybe my heart will have turned to stone and it will be time for me to stop. Donors often ask me to tell their student's background stories but I can't tell them all because I find it difficult and intrusive to ask them to relive all their past traumas. They will tell me, if they want, in their own time and I will try to be there to listen. Those stories related here, with their permission, have been told to me over ten or more years of our quietly talking together. It is painful for them to relate, and it is often difficult for me to listen without becoming deeply upset. As I said, Ethiopians don't cry, but silent tears are both painful and moving to witness.

I try not to allow any photograph be published with our children in rags or with any visible disabilities. I want to show them at their best and brightest, yes positively smiling and shining - probably with borrowed "best" clothes. That is a dignity they deserve. I am not looking for sympathy for them or emotional donors, what I do and for whom I do it surely deserves support on its own merit.

Let me assure all from the bottom of my heart that at A-CET I know we are open and honest, we are caring, helpful, flexible and try to be non-judgmental. Building on my decades of overseas experience, we work with a local organisation run by our ex-students who in their turn work through local communities, building trust. The communities are asked what they want and we try to give them those assets to carry it out themselves. So real control is delegated right down to the communities and the rural elementary schools we help build belong to them. I find this all immeasurably fulfilling and deeply humbling. This is a daunting and very great responsibility. I can see that our support is producing incredible life changing results, but often there is far more to do than our minimal cash allows. Without doubt our most important ingredient is our care and love. In a country where so few families have parents, to know that others love and care for you is a vital and important anchor for these often abandoned youngsters. In the UK A-CET continues to have no paid staff and is governed by a small board of volunteer trustees - which includes Dame Claire and our two inspirational young Ethiopians Bisrat and Sammy. All our trustees, unpaid, bring their time, their passion, their experience and above all their common sense towards A-CET.

Once on a local Ethiopian flight back to the capital I was asked by an Arab trader if I was an investor. Reluctant and shy to answer, eventually I agreed, *"Yes I invest in youngsters"*. The puzzled questioner wanted to know about the returns. *"The highest,"* I replied, *"but mine's a very long-term investment"*. No comment or reply for the rest of the one hour flight.

> *Birhan Woldu, 1984 famine survivor with her Diploma in Agriculture and degree in Nursing, now working as a nurse writes:*
>
> *"We are a big country and when there is famine in one part there can be plenty of food in another. So we need better infrastructure and communications to be able to move food around to wherever it is needed. Above all we need an education to manage this ourselves. We Ethiopians are an intelligent, tough and hard working people with a culture going back thousands of years, and all of us want an education. For example my father is a farmer but he is not educated. With my diploma I have been able to show him better ways to farm more efficiently and get better yields".*

A-CET is increasingly moving towards being more Ethiopian managed, which is how I believe it should be. All our activities in Ethiopia, within our policy guidelines, are initiated, led and managed by Ethiopians. A-CET is developing into a self-perpetuating and sustaining charity of its own, yet the more we do the more that it seems there is to do.

It seems appropriate to close this book with the charity Ethiopian Youth Educational Support quote from Bisrat Mesfin, Chief Executive and Chair of (EYES), A-CET's Ethiopian national implementing partner and also an A-CET Trustee:

"Our children are both our priority and most important asset"

With Afghan companion Qudous
in Peshawar, Pakistan

Typical mule train in
Afghan pass

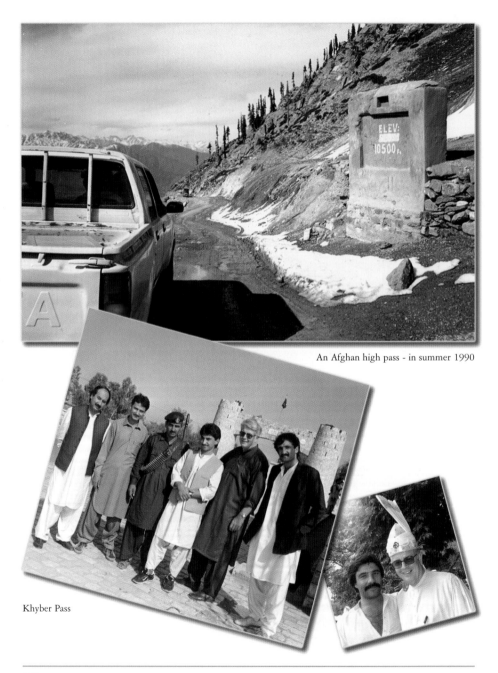

An Afghan high pass - in summer 1990

Khyber Pass

Relaxing at Muree - Christmas 1990

Somalia communication centre - 1992

Mekelle - 1995

Red Cross office in Melcelle 1995 with Solomon Mekonnen

Afar food distribution Elidar - 1994

Relief food stocks at Adigudom

Typical road to a distribution
centre - Wajirat 1995

In Afar, food distribution was often by camel - 1993

Gumselasa dam nearing completion

Adigudom Red Cross Food
distribution office with Head of
Delegation Hannes Hauksson
and his wife - 1996

With Red Cross recording officer Solomon Mekonnen - 1995

Building Gumselasa Micro dam slipway - 1995

Prince, Ysakor and Tammy eat their morning porridge before school - 1994. These were early pre- A-CET students.

Bisrat Mesfin 17th Birthday - 1995

Dubti Red Cross Football
Team, Afar - 1993

With visiting old school friend Roger and (the late) Bishop Makarios in - 1994

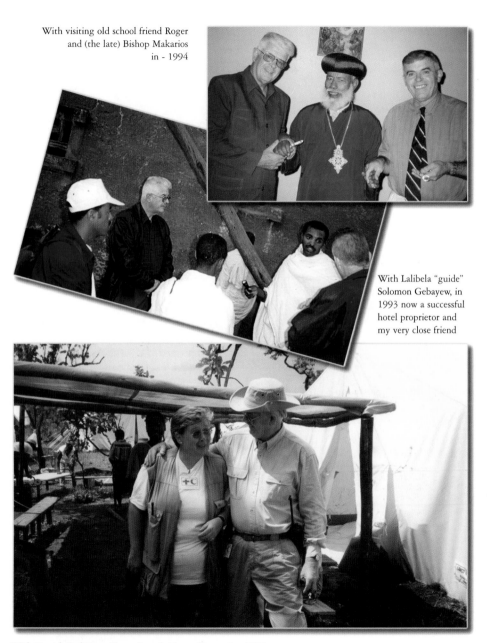

With Lalibela "guide" Solomon Gebayew, in 1993 now a successful hotel proprietor and my very close friend

With Finnish Red Cross Nurse, Lugufu Camp, Tanzamia - 1997

Enjoying a joke with
Gumselasa Student in half
built classroom

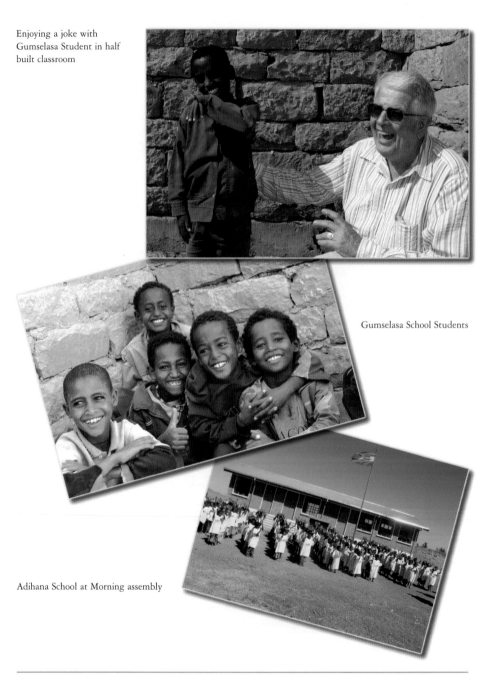

Gumselasa School Students

Adihana School at Morning assembly

HH Abba Paulos V, Patriarch Ethiopian Orthodox Church opens new Abinet church school - 2010

President Tsegay Berhe presents
award, Mekelle - 2010

EYES Patron, HE Ambassador Dr Kassa Gebrehiwot, retired Commissioner for Human Rights - 2009

Meeting with Ato Seyoum
Mesfin, Minister of Foreign
Affairs, accompanied by Patron
HE Ambassador Dr Kassa

With Bisrat and Sir Bob in Mekelle - 2009

Ex students Yemane and Tammy, both are employed, married and with their first sons

Birhan and Bisrat on the Oprah Winfrey Show - 2004
"Children who changed the World"

Birhan and Bisrat at Live 8 in
London 2005 whilst Madonna Sings

With Ezana Asfaw

With Haftom Gilay "Moko"

With Civil Engineering
undergraduate Kokob

Ex student Tammy now drives big trucks

With Binyam aged 15, I was
present at his birth in 1994

Tamrat, Diploma student, plays the
saxaphone in a night club

A-CET trustees at Honorary
Doctorate ceremony at DeMontfort
University Leicester for Dame Claire with
her mother and Sammy in 2009

With Bisrat Mesfin and
Rahel - 2010

EYES Band play "Feed the World"
with Nurse Brhan holding Ethiopian
national Flag

179

Ceremony at new school Hagere Selam - 2009

Typical new basically furnished classroom - Adihana

Top students win awards

Happy Students

School under construction
- Adi' baekel

Birhan, Sir Bob, Dame Claire and HE, Regional President Tsegay Berhe - Nov 2009

VALUABLE WORK: David Stables talks through an interpreter to one of the students in Africa his charity has helped to educate

Education charity's book-keeping put to good account

A SMALL Leicester charity has won a sixth of its annual income in a national accountancy award.

The African Children's Educational Trust spends £12,000 a year helping to educate students in Ethiopia, Sierra Leone, Kenya and Tanzania.

The trust won £2,000 for its "model" annual report in this year's Charities' Annual Report

and Accounts Award (CARAA).

Organised by the Institute of Chartered Accountants and the Charities Aid Foundation, the awards are designed to encourage charities to transform their report and accounts into effective communication tools.

The prize money could pay for another 16 students for one year, says the chairman of the trustees, David Stables, but he will

probably add 12 to the existing 27, explaining: "We have to have something in reserve.

"If you take someone on, you can't drop them after a year – it has to be for the next 10 years."

Mr Stables, warden of the Friends Meeting House, in Queen's Road, has worked overseas for most of his life.

He has been involved with charities such as the Interna-

tional Red Cross and Care International.

He registered A-CET as a charity after returning to the UK three years ago.

"I wanted to continue helping with education, but couldn't afford to do it on my own. Leicester people have been very generous and supportive."

Mr Stables can be contacted on 07041-210982

~~Award won~~

LM/21
THURSDAY, MAY 15, 2008   **NEWS**   LEICESTER MERCURY **17**

NOMINATION: DAVID IS UP FOR AN AWARD AFTER STARTING TRUST WHEN HE RETIRED

Charity founder an inspiration

CHAIRMAN: David Stables

When most people retire, they look forward to putting their feet up - not David Stables.

Instead of a well-earned rest, the charity worker continued his good work, this time helping to transform thousands of children's lives in Africa.

Working from his Evington home, with no salary and living

by ZEENAT SABUR

off his state pension, he is chief executive and chairman of trustees of African Children's Educational Trust (A-CET).

Today, it supports the education of more than 2,000 children in Ethiopia.

It receives no Government funding and has raised £269,000 in more than 20 countries.

David's efforts have seen him nominated as one of Britain's most inspiring fund-raisers.

David started A-CET after retiring from the Red Cross, aged 60, in 1997.

He said: "I was horrified at the poverty in Africa and felt education could change the lives of the people there and give them a better future.

"Working for A-CET is the best

thing I have ever done and I wish now I'd retired earlier.

"I'm very excited to be nominated. It is a wonderful feeling."

Mr Stables was nominated by Samuel Assesa, a trustee of the charity.

He said: "I believe David's undying passion and belief in A-CET's cause has made him the most inspiring fund-raiser with such credible results."

The award was set up in memory of Jane Tomlinson who raised more than £1.75 million for cancer charities before she died of the disease in 2007.

The winner will be announced on June 11 and will receive £20,000 for their chosen charity.

FOR MORE INFORMATION, GO TO
www.a-cet.org

Charity win 'is wonderful'

A LEICESTER charity which helps disadvantaged young Africans has won first place in an annual award.

The African Children's Educational Trust was recognised at the Charities' Annual Report and Accounts Awards.

The city charity generates £12,000 and supports 27 students on average every year.

Its annual report and accounts were said to be a model for such small organisations.

David Stables, the trust's chairman, said: "This award is nothing short of wonderful. It will be used to fully support 16 children in their studies for another year, as we are entirely dependent on private voluntary support and have no paid staff and minimal overheads.

"Our work aims to help African young people live fuller and more productive lives through education so that they can support themselves and their families. Already we have more than 40 beneficiary students in Ethiopia and some of our older graduates are in employment."

THE I
CH

Charity man in line for award

THE founder of a charity which provides educational opportunities for young people in Africa has been honoured with a national award.

David Stables, of Leicester charity the African Children's Educational Trust (A-CET) was given a special commendation by judges for the Beacon Prize 2006.

Mr Stables was nominated for his "tireless and selfless" contribution over eight years in providing educational support to more than 2,000 vulnerable orphans and abandoned or disabled children in Ethiopia.

His star student is Birhan Woldu, the Ethiopian girl, who became the face of Live 8 last year, when she appeared on stage with Bob Geldof and Madonna. She graduated from college last week.

DELIGHT: David Stables

Mr Stables said: "On behalf of A-CET, I am delighted to receive this high commendation from the Beacon Fellowship. I hope it will inspire others to support our work."

Emily Stonor, chief executive of Beacon, said: "Being highly commended is a truly remarkable accomplishment and to be judged alongside prize winners such as The Big Issue founder John Bird and safety campaigners Paul and Diana Lamplugh is a recognition of David Stables achievement for A-CET.

"We are delighted to acknowledge David's contribution to charity and we hope his success will be an inspiration to others."

The overall winner of the prize, to be announced at a ceremony in November, will be given £30,000 to invest in a charity of their choice. For more information, visit: **www.beaconfellowship.org.uk** www.a-cet.org

caraa

Charities' Annual Report and Accounts Awards

2002 Charities' Annual Report and Accounts Awards

Sponsored by

The Institute of Chartered Accountants in England & Wales
and CAF (Charities Aid Foundation)

Second in Category: Income below £100,000

African Children's Educational Trust

Chairman of the Judges
Alderman Sir Brian Jenkins, GBE, FCA

Presented at Chartered Accountants' Hall 23 April 2002

The Charity Awards 2003

INTERNATIONAL AID AND DEVELOPMENT CATEGORY

COMMENDED

African Children's Educational Trust

signed on behalf of the judges, Heather Lamont, Editor *Charity Finance*

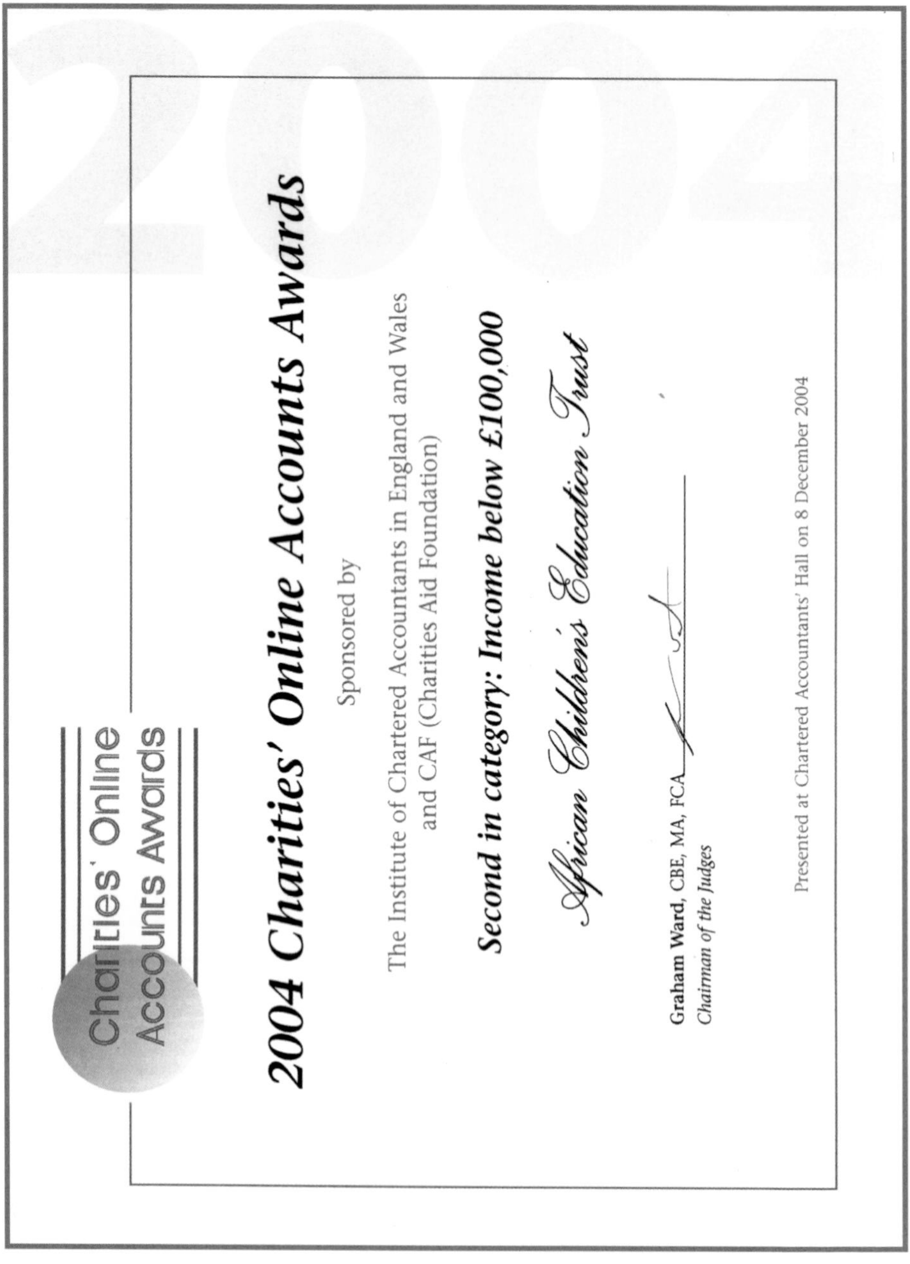

Charities' Online
Accounts Awards

2004

2004 Charities' Online Accounts Awards

Sponsored by

The Institute of Chartered Accountants in England and Wales
and CAF (Charities Aid Foundation)

Second in category: Income below £100,000

African Childrens' Education Trust

Graham Ward, CBE, MA, FCA
Chairman of the Judges

Presented at Chartered Accountants' Hall on 8 December 2004

THE BEACON FELLOWSHIP
CHARITABLE TRUST

HIGHLY COMMENDED

Certificate is Awarded to

David Stables

THIS IS AWARDED IN RECOGNITION OF YOUR
OUTSTANDING CONTRIBUTION TO CHARITABLE AND
SOCIAL CAUSES. YOU WERE HIGHLY COMMENDED
IN THE CATEGORY OF

New Initiatives

Emily Stoner
Chief Executive

Martyn Lewis
Chairman of the Trustees

The Government of National Regional State of Tigrai

Certificate of Appreciation

This certificate of appreciation is awarded to Mr. David Graham Stables for his excellent work and dedication to contribute in to the socio-economic development of Tigrai Regional State through education. Mr. David who is the founder of A-CET has targeted to help the vulnerable children to make them self sustained in life through quality education. He has constructed several primary schools and simultaneously serves the children with counseling, guidance, and other social skill activities. He is also well known by his total commitment to the success of the children and has ardently contributed Ethiopia/Tigrai since 1993 in various programs. He has served in the Red Cross Society and worked in close cooperation with different sector of the Region. In using his humanitarian and professional experience, he has spent more than 18 year of his life in Ethiopia /Tigrai. He is therefore endowed with this Reward to strongly appreciate his kind work and endless effort to bring social developments in Tigrai.

With best regards

Tsegay Berhe
President

June 20/2010

Chapter 12 - Afterword

I have seen and lived through some unpleasant things perpetrated by some distinctly unsavoury people - not always in Africa. So why do I work in and for Ethiopia? Well why anywhere? Ultimately it must always be the people and their culture, with the food and the environment an added bonus. I have the deepest respect and admiration for this stoic, gentle and cultured people that I have come to know and work with. I admire Ethiopians' calm dignity, their kind selflessness; their ever courteous and, above all, open honesty, which endear themselves totally to me. Unashamedly I admit to a deep love for Ethiopia and its people. Trying to involve myself and understand these hard working, intelligent and justifiably proud and noble people, I count myself blessed that I can be of some use by helping offer educational support in, I hope, a sensitive respectful way that is acceptable to them.

When will the "developed" or western world ever allow Africa to compete fairly? When can ethnic or tribal distrusts be set aside? I believe Ethiopia has so much admirable potential young talent, with that ability to rise up again to its respected great international status it held so many thousands of years ago. Much has been written and made of the evils of colonialism and how slavery "exported" its best potential out of the continent. Yet today we have economic imperialism and a form of slavery where the western world entices all Africa's best brains and highly skilled potential to work overseas. The US Diversity Lottery (DV) lottery is not unique and we in the UK must also bear some blame for inducing those top achievers abroad. It is an international disgrace that these youngsters have to go abroad to earn a better income, albeit often in some menial post. A-CET has only "lost" one graduate to the US, but unless the goal posts change, I fear it could be many more. The western world must realise that 'our way' may not be 'their way' and that it should stop telling others how to think and what to do. I believe in time it can and will change, if and when the western world allows, or is no longer in a position to enforce so much "conditional" aid in this current unfair and biased situation.

The politicians may make all the slick sound-bites, but through A-CET and its Ethiopian partner EYES, we are actually doing something. As we like to say *"we do it, not just talk about it"*. It may sound rather arrogant to say we are actively supporting what can be a potential educational renaissance yet our contribution may be only a very small pebble in the big pond. I am no lobbyist nor do I feel able to influence politicians or governments, so let me do what I do best, organising and supporting education. Big multi million projects run by self perpetuating agencies do so much harm, create their own dependency and are so wasteful of resources it makes me weep with frustration. Whilst we try to distance ourselves from them, sadly our successes create jealousies. Our projects and even our successful students (like Birhan Woldu) are photographed and used by other agencies as their projects. "Development aid" can be a very dirty cut-throat business as all compete for the donors support. I am no salesman and an abysmally reticent fund-raiser, but I believe passionately that with a good practical and focussed practical education, people can have that potential to change the world in their small way to produce big results. To be pragmatic and have this dream may sound contradictory but let me contribute to it as best I am able - for as long as I can. It is my honour to use my organisational skills, my ability to motivate and encourage and to offer an unbounded caring love for these often fatherless youngsters. Does this sound a bit smug? Let not any pride in these achievements make me become like those pretentious pompous bluffers I find so difficult to accept.

I admit to many faults and making so many mistakes, although I have hopefully learnt from them. Some events in my past give me no cause for pride. To others at times I may have seemed rather distant even arrogant. I admit to shyness in strange company, perhaps essentially out of an inherent sense of insecurity. I do not brim with self-confidence, although ironically I know I'm good at inspiring and cultivating it in others. Essentially I have always believed that life should be fun for all of us. Under the guise of survival or protecting others, to my eternal shame, I have not always reacted properly to known wrongs, and that I must live with. With all my faults, imperfections, intolerances, to be felt accepted in Ethiopia and by most Ethiopians, is humbling and a source of continual wonder to me.

I run no car, (most people in the UK say that they are sorry that I can't drive), and I still live in happy contentment in my small, quiet council flat surrounded by trees and grassy lawns. I believe very few in our block have any idea I run a charity or what I do and I'm happy to keep it that way. Despite in the past having earned good salaries, now it seems I'm always juggling bank overdrafts and credit cards and have never managed to accumulate any savings. There always seem to be others far more in need. My pockets are always empty, yet I get by on my modest state pension. I am supposedly classed as materially poor, although I set little store by such measures. I am blessed with reasonable health and the richness of wonderful friends. My life and struggles have made me quite tough and I'm no quitter. What I do and what successes I have, I owe to those who support me and in this I'm fortunate. I deeply value personal relationships and long-term mutual trust. I accept I'm not inherently right about many things and many more things I don't fully comprehend, so why should I feel I need to make any comment? I find it difficult to accept many of the world's inherent injustices yet I now feel more at peace with myself than ever in my life. I am, by choice, still divorced and alone, although I never feel alone. I've tried not to include too many quotes or platitudes in this book. Many names are not included here and some have been changed, although I am ever grateful to those great and good I have met and learnt from. I've tried to be kind to those referred to in less than complimentary terms. They may know who they are, and if the cap fits, so be it. No excuses, our lives are far too short. All is forgiven - if perhaps not forgotten!

Much large scale "aid" is far too "conditional" and has done little to improve anything in the developing world. On a large scale it often makes things worse, very much worse. It undermines governments, it has created dependency, it has destroyed local initiatives, it unbalances rates and it fosters and feeds corruption with the potential to undermine legitimate governments.

But ever the "half full glass" optimist, I count myself to be so very lucky and fortunate and in so many ways privileged to have been accepted in others lives. I have met some really lovely admirable people whom I greatly respect.

On that final day of reckoning, I may not have been such a "good" man, not everything I can be proud of. My personal academic record has been a disappointment to me, but I measure my achievements through those I've helped, a sort of education by proxy. As our students get their Bachelors, Masters and Doctors I can only tell my students I am QBE - qualified by experience, perhaps not their best role model. I've done my best and try to treat everybody fairly and with respect. I can be intolerant of fools and, with still so much to do, I can be impatient, probably not the best quality for working in Africa. I hope I have not taken myself too seriously, as Oscar Wilde said, *"life is too short"*. We may all rather pompously like to think we made a difference for the better, but only others can judge that.

How do you measure change or impact? I accept we must measure and report on things and I enjoy numbers and statistics although I am always rather wary of them as so easy to manipulate. It was Josef Stalin who said *"When you start to believe your own statistics then you've lost"* - and he should have known. School academic results are only one way but can never tell the full story. How do you measure how a whole village changes and becomes more positive and supportive of education? How do you measure how youngsters grow from shuffling down-cast youths into mature, confident, healthy, bright-eyed young men and women visibly walking tall. How can you ever manage how they feel about themselves, their higher aspirations and their better futures? Only decades can tell.

For myself I've long since given up thinking I can change the world, but I do believe that I have helped some live better lives, to have brighter futures with more opportunities. That this has been recognized by Ethiopia in my being receiving a certificate of appreciation from Mr Tsegay Berhe, Tigrai Regional President (see page 190) I deeply value.

And my being offered Honorary Ethiopian Citizenship is indeed a great honour. My colleagues in Afghanistan were right; I am at heart more of an "African man".

Closing quote from my long-time friend and casual driver in Addis Abeba I've known as *"City boy"* as the attractions of the capital seem to be too much to entice him to come to work in the Tigrai Region full-time: *"I like you so much David"*, [pause ... my puzzled looks], *"because you're so antique!"*

Thanks sincerely for your time. I hope you enjoyed your read as much as I did in its writing; although on completion I must admit to feeling rather naked in a very public place. As I grow older, let me do so with some grace and dignity - as did my Mother.

"Let my voice be heard by all my people. I am going in the quest of wisdom and learning. My spirit impels me to find out where they are to be had, for I am smitten with the lack of wisdom and I feel drawn as by a leash towards learning.

Learning is better than treasures of silver and gold, better than all that has been created on earth. And afterward what can be compared to learning?

God will grant that all I have learned from you [King Solomon] may bear fruit in the soul of those my people. I was ignorant and through you I have learnt wisdom.

Princess Makeda, later Queen of Sheba (Saba) 9th century BC

Notes and Abbreviations

Abyssinia	Previous name for Ethiopia (also historically sometimes referred to as Land of Punt)
A-CET	African Children's Educational Trust, a charity registered in England & Wales
ADC	Aide de Camp (Military term for personal assistant to President or high personage)
APC	Armoured Personnel Carrier (military)
	All People's Congress (Sierra Leone political party)
Ato	Mister (title in Ethiopia)
BESO	British Executive Services Overseas, a volunteer organization, now subsumed by VSO
Birr	Ethiopian currency, literally silver
BAOR	British Army on the Rhine
CAB	Citizen's Advice Bureau
CBC	Canadian Broadcasting Corporation
CO	Commanding Officer in Military
Derg	Literally Ethiopian for "committee". The Soviet backed Marxist ruling body from 1974 - 92
Dejatch	Ethiopian Prince
DfID	UK Department for International Development, before Overseas Development Administration (ODA)
DV	US Diversity Visa, an application system for those applying for Immigration to work in USA
ERCS	Ethiopian Red Cross Society
Expat	Expatriate, Foreigner, Stranger, Frank (Afghan), Ferengi (Ethiopian), Mzungu (Swahili), Palangi (Polynesian)
EYES	Ethiopian Youth Educational Support, a charity registered in Ethiopia
Humvee	US military all terrain jeep, very large
KAF	Kenyan Air Force
KAR	King's African Rifles, later became Kenyan Army Regiment
kipande	Kenyan Identity Card (old style)
kikoi	Kenyan wrap round cloth worn in hot climates
Krio	Language used in Sierra Leone

Laterite	Red earth road found in much of Africa
Leones	Sierra Leone currency
NFD	Northern Frontier District, Kenya
NGO	Non-governmental organization, termed often used overseas for charities
Poda poda	Sierra Leonean mini-bus
Ras	An Ethiopian Duke, usually a member of the royal family
Shifta	Commonly accepted as Somali Cattle Rustlers
SLOF	Sierra Leone Oxygen Factory
SLPP	Sierra Leone Peoples Party
TANZAM	Now TAZARA, Tanzania to Zambia Railway, built and operated by the Chinese
TPLF	Tigrean People's Liberation Front
TVET	Technical & Vocational Education Training (Ethiopian secondary college, post Grade 10)
UNICEF	United Nations Children's Fund
UNHCR	United Nations High Commissioner for Refugees
UTA	Union des Transport Aeriens - French independent airline flying in Africa, now defunct
VSO	Voluntary Services Overseas
wadi	Dry river bed, soft sand also liable to quick flooding
WFP	World Food Programme

GEEZ/AMHARIC ALPHABET

	ä	u	i	a	e	ï	o		ä	u	i	a	e	ï	o
h	ህ	ሁ	ሂ	ሃ	ሄ	ህ	ሆ	h	ከ	ኩ	ኪ	ካ	ኬ	ክ	ኮ
l	ለ	ሉ	ሊ	ላ	ሌ	ል	ሎ	w	ወ	ዉ	ዊ	ዋ	ዌ	ው	ዎ
h	ሐ	ሑ	ሒ	ሓ	ሔ	ሕ	ሖ	a	ዐ	ዑ	ዒ	ዓ	ዔ	ዕ	ዖ
m	መ	ሙ	ሚ	ማ	ሜ	ም	ሞ	z	ዘ	ዙ	ዚ	ዛ	ዜ	ዝ	ዞ
s	ሠ	ሡ	ሢ	ሣ	ሤ	ሥ	ሦ	zh	ዠ	ዡ	ዢ	ዣ	ዤ	ዥ	ዦ
r	ረ	ሩ	ሪ	ራ	ሬ	ር	ሮ	y	የ	ዩ	ዪ	ያ	ዬ	ይ	ዮ
s	ሰ	ሱ	ሲ	ሳ	ሴ	ስ	ሶ	d	ደ	ዱ	ዲ	ዳ	ዴ	ድ	ዶ
sh	ሸ	ሹ	ሺ	ሻ	ሼ	ሽ	ሾ	j	ጀ	ጁ	ጂ	ጃ	ጄ	ጅ	ጆ
q	ቀ	ቁ	ቂ	ቃ	ቄ	ቅ	ቆ	g	ገ	ጉ	ጊ	ጋ	ጌ	ግ	ጎ
b	በ	ቡ	ቢ	ባ	ቤ	ብ	ቦ	t'	ጠ	ጡ	ጢ	ጣ	ጤ	ጥ	ጦ
t	ተ	ቱ	ቲ	ታ	ቴ	ት	ቶ	ch'	ጨ	ጩ	ጪ	ጫ	ጬ	ጭ	ጮ
ch	ቸ	ቹ	ቺ	ቻ	ቼ	ች	ቾ	p'	ጰ	ጱ	ጲ	ጳ	ጴ	ጵ	ጶ
h	ኀ	ኁ	ኂ	ኃ	ኄ	ኅ	ኆ	s'	ጸ	ጹ	ጺ	ጻ	ጼ	ጽ	ጾ
n	ነ	ኑ	ኒ	ና	ኔ	ን	ኖ	s'	ፀ	ፁ	ፂ	ፃ	ፄ	ፅ	ፆ
ñ	ኘ	ኙ	ኚ	ኛ	ኜ	ኝ	ኞ	f	ፈ	ፉ	ፊ	ፋ	ፌ	ፍ	ፎ
a	አ	ኡ	ኢ	ኣ	ኤ	እ	ኦ	p	ፐ	ፑ	ፒ	ፓ	ፔ	ፕ	ፖ
k	ከ	ኩ	ኪ	ካ	ኬ	ክ	ኮ								

Note on spelling

The Ethiopian alphabet has nearly three hundred characters (including seven vowels), so it is possible to have many English translations that are all acceptable. I have used what I consider easiest to understand, although others may have other interpretations. We can all be correct.

If you found this book interesting you may like to read the following:

A long way home by Ishmael Beah - a Sierra Leone child soldier's story articulate and evocative

Barefoot Emperor by Philip Marsden - Emperor Tewodrus II's life

Chains of Heaven by Philip Marsden - An Ethiopian travelogue, sensitive and beautifully written

Emperor by Ryszard Kapuscinski - Emperor Haile Selassie's life

Garbage King by Elizabeth Laird - an evocative account of street children's life in Addis Abeba

Geldof in Africa by Bob Geldof - a beautifully written perceptive and amusing collection of African observations belying Bob's deep love of Africa

"Is that it?" by Bob Geldof

Moving Mountains by Claire Bertschinger - our own Trustees life story as a nurse with the Red Cross

Race Against Time by Stephen Lewis - the AIDS pandemic in Africa, a disturbing read

Trouble with Africa by Robert Calderisi - Why foreign aid isn't working, knowledgeable

War Games by Linda Polman - Aid and war in modern times, read this and you may never donate again

White Man's Burden by William Easterly - Why foreign aid has done so little good, good guidelines

"A riveting read from a great humanitarian" - Oliver Harvey, Chief Feature Writer, The Sun

For an impassioned account of how one man's drive and determination has effectively inspired thousands of vulnerable young Ethiopians to positively change their own lives through access to better education. I heartily commend you to read this book - and support A-CET's worthwhile cause!" - Dr Dame Claire Bertschinger

Published by the African Children's Educational Trust (A-CET)
Registered Charity 1066869 (England & Wales)
© David G Stables
PO Box 8390, Leicester LE5 4YD,
ISBN 978-0-9557041-1-6

Designed and printed by Flexpress
6 Coal Cart Road, Interchange, Birstall, Leicester LE4 3BY
Telephone: 0116 222 2223 Website: www.flexpress.co.uk

October 2010